# THE LOBSTER KIDS' GUIDE TO EXPLORING LAS VEGAS

BY HEIDI KNAPP RINELLA

Lobster Press™

Rinella, Heidi Knapp, 1956-
The Lobster Kids' Guide to Exploring Las Vegas: 12 Months of Fun!


Published by
Lobster Press™
1620 Sherbrooke St. W., Suites C & D
Montréal, Québec H3H 1C9
Tel. (514) 904-1100, Fax (514) 904-1101
www.lobsterpress.com

Publisher: Alison Fripp
Editor: Bob Kirner
Assistant Editor: Alison Fischer
Copy Editor: Frances Purslow
Cover and Illustrations: Christine Battuz
Icons: Christiane Beauregard and Josée Masse
Layout and Design: Olivier Lasser

Distribution:

In the United States
Advanced Global Distribution Services
5880 Oberlin Drive, Suite 400
San Diego, CA 92121
Tel. (858) 457-2500
Fax (858) 812-6476

In Canada
Raincoast Books
9050 Shaughnessey St.
Vancouver, BC V6P 6E5
Tel. 1-800-663-5714
Fax 1-800-565-3770

We acknowledge the financial support of the Government of Canada through the Book Publishing Industry Development Program (BPIDP) for our publishing activities.

National Library of Canada Cataloguing in Publication Data

Rinella, Heidi Knapp, 1956-
The Lobster kids' guide to exploring las vegas: 12 months of fun!

Includes Index.
ISBN 1-894222-29-6

1. Family recreation—Nevada—Las Vegas—Guidebooks. 2. Children—Travel—Nevada—Las Vegas—Guidebooks. 3. Amusements—Nevada—Las Vegas—Guidebooks. 4. Las Vegas (Nev.)—Guidebooks. I. Christine Battuz II. Kirner, Bob, 1959– III. Title.

F849.L35R55 2001 917.93'1350434 C2001-900047-2

Printed and bound in Canada

# *Table of Contents*

# *Author's Introduction*

May you and your families have as much fun exploring the Las Vegas Valley as my family did while researching this book.

When I agreed to write it, we were fairly new to Las Vegas, but I thought we knew most of the area's high points. Months later, I realized how wrong I had been. And in the interim, we got to visit places missed by most tourists and many long-time residents.

Las Vegas is known for its slot machines, but more interesting to families are the many spots that give visitors a taste of the area's breathtaking environment and colorful history. There's a rich diversity in the Las Vegas Valley that shouldn't be overlooked. If you're a visitor, try to see a few sites that aren't in the tourist brochures. If you live here, delve in and learn all about your city through the eyes of your kids.

I'd like to express my thanks to my editor, Bob Kirner, for his guidance and especially his patience, and to the rest of the Lobster Press™ staff for giving me the opportunity to write this book.

I thank my mother, Jean Knapp, and late father, Eugene Knapp, who gave me a lifetime of fun, educational opportunities and fostered the adventurous spirit that made exploring the sites mentioned in this book a joy.

But foremost I'd like to thank my daughter Aubrey, who was my chief companion while researching this book; my daughter Aynsley, who lent support in ways she may never understand; and especially my husband and best friend Frank, for his unwavering good nature, cooperation, support and deep well of tolerance. I love you all.

HEIDI KNAPP RINELLA

# *A Word from the Publisher*

Lobster Press™ published its first book, *The Lobster Kids' Guide to Exploring Montréal* in 1998. Since then, the Kids' City Explorers Series has grown and now includes guides to other major Canadian cities. Due to the resounding success of the Canadian series, this year Lobster Press™ is publishing books for families exploring cities in the United States.

Whether you're a tourist, resident, parent or teacher, this book is a complete resource of things to do and see with kids in the Las Vegas area. It's jam-packed with valuable, timesaving information and great ideas for outings.

Heidi Knapp Rinella and her family visited the sites in this guide in 2000-2001. All information provided has been verified. However, since prices and business hours are subject to change, call ahead to avoid disappointment. Please accept our apologies in advance for any inconvenience you may encounter.

To get the most out of this guide, please familiarize yourself with our "Lobster Rating System" and table of icons. These features let you know what Heidi's family thought of each site and what amenities are available. Please note that traveling distances to the sites were determined from McCarran International Airport.

If you have comments about this book, visit our website and complete our on-line survey. Let us know if we've missed your family's favorite destination and we'll include it in the next edition!

One last word: Please be careful when you and your children visit the sites from the guide. Neither Lobster Press™ nor the author can be held responsible for any accidents that might occur.

Enjoy! And watch for the other books in the Kids' City Explorers Series. Now available: Boston, Chicago, San Francisco and Seattle. Coming in 2002: Halifax, Miami, New Orleans, Québec City and San Diego.

FROM THE GANG AT LOBSTER PRESS™

# *The Lobster Rating System*

We thought it would be helpful if you knew what Heidi Knapp Rinella and her family thought about the sites in this book before you head off to visit them. They rated every attraction and activity they visited for its:

- ☞ enjoyment level for children
- ☞ learning opportunities for children
- ☞ accessibility from McCarran International Airport
- ☞ costs and value for the money

A one-lobster rating: Good attraction.

A two-lobster rating: Very good attraction.

A three-lobster rating: Excellent attraction.

Not fitting some of the criteria, and subsequently not rated, are green spaces and various similar, nearby or other attractions.

# *Table of Icons*

These facilities and/or activities are represented by the following icons:

Beach

Bicycling

Birthday parties

Bus stop

Hiking

Information center

In-line skating

Parking

Picnic tables

Playgrounds

Restaurant/ snack bar

Restrooms

Swimming

Telephone

Wheelchair/stroller accessible

Wildlife watching

CHAPTER 1

# LOCAL ATTRACTIONS

# *Introduction*

There's no other city in the world that can top the variety of unique (and sometimes downright campy) attractions in Las Vegas.

Families are especially lucky—the 1989 debut of the volcano at the Mirage heralded an era of elaborate attractions (most of them free), with casinos trying desperately to outdo each other. Despite the presence of casino gaming, which is by law off-limits to kids, Las Vegas has lots for families. Resort owners recognizing the dawning of a new era, where adults traveling for business or pleasure often have children in town, met the challenge by providing something for the younger set.

In this chapter, you'll find the most noteworthy attractions in Las Vegas, from the towering Stratosphere to a bubbling volcano, with a pirate battle in between. Most of them are free and all are worth visiting, if for no other reason than to tell the unbelieving folks back home.

# *An Eiffel Experience in Vegas*
# EIFFEL TOWER

**Paris, 3665 Las Vegas Blvd. S., Las Vegas**
**(702) 946-7000**
**www.paris-lv.com**

It may only be half the size of the original in the other Paris, but zip to the top of the Eiffel Tower in Las Vegas—and chances are you'll be awed.

The top of the tower is reached by smooth, quiet elevators and is a great vantage point to see Las Vegas, especially if the soaring height of the Stratosphere (page 22) is too much for you. The view is undeniably gorgeous and the top of the tower's a perfect spot for viewing the Fountains of Bellagio show (page 27).

The tower's observation platform is enclosed in heavy mesh, so you don't have to worry about those little citizens of Paris. Peepholes have been thoughtfully provided for those who wish to poke their cameras through for that perfect photo. You'll learn trivia about the real Eiffel Tower (the Las Vegas version is an exact replica), such as how many bolts were used and the differences in construction technique between the real thing and this copy.

There's a restaurant halfway up the tower if you need an energy boost. At the base of the tower, nearly all that the City of Light has to offer is available.

**SEASONS AND TIMES**

➛ Year-round: Daily, 9 am—1 am.

**COST**

➛ Adults $9, seniors $7, under 5 free.

**GETTING THERE**

➛ By car, take I-15 north to the Flamingo Rd. E. Exit. Travel east on Flamingo to Las Vegas Blvd. and turn south. Paris will be on your left (just look for the Eiffel Tower). Free parking on site. About 15 minutes from McCarran International Airport.

➛ By public transit, take city bus route 301. It stops along Las Vegas Blvd.

**NEARBY**

➛ Bally's, Bellagio, Aladdin.

**COMMENT**

➛ This is a great one to attend in conjunction with the Fountains at the Bellagio, especially if you can time it to see the fountain show from the tower. Plan a 1-hour visit.

## *Hail Caesar!*
## FORUM SHOPS

**Caesars Palace, 3500 Las Vegas Blvd. S., Las Vegas**
**(702) 893-4800**
**www.caesars.com**

Not one, but two free shows await you in the Forum Shops at Caesars Palace. Both are mesmerizing for even the most jaded kids.

The original is the Fountain Festival, which is near the Caesars Palace entrance to the Shops. There, Bacchus, the Greek god of wine, holds court. His animated robotic show, based on myths of the ancient gods, involves lots of crowd-pleasing lasers and sound effects.

But Neptune isn't going to be outdone by Bacchus. Another story—this time about a conflict among the gods—unfolds during the Lost City of Atlantis Show near the farthest reaches of the Shops. The show comes complete with lighting strikes, fire and crashing sound effects. It might be a little frightening for smaller tots, but the eight-and-up crowd will love it. Adjacent to the action is a 50,000-gallon saltwater aquarium filled with vibrant tropical fish.

Another benefit is the Forum Shops—decorated with Roman columns and arches, statues and fountains, and a ceiling that reflects how the sky changes over the course of a day. There are more than 100 restaurants and shops, including a big FAO Schwarz toy store where kids enter through a Trojan horse.

**SEASONS AND TIMES**

➛ Fountain Festival: Year-round, Sun—Thu, 10 am—11 pm; Fri—Sat, 10 am—midnight. Lost City of Atlantis: Year-round, Sun—Thu, 11 am—11 pm; Fri—Sat, 10 am—midnight. Both shows start every hour on the hour.

**COST**

➛ Free.

**GETTING THERE**

➛ By car, take I-15 N. to the Flamingo Rd. E. Exit. Travel east on Flamingo to Las Vegas Blvd. and turn north. Free parking on site. About 15 minutes from McCarran International Airport.

➛ By public transit, take city bus route 301. It stops along Las Vegas Blvd.

**NEARBY**

➛ Bellagio, Flamingo Hilton, Mirage.

**COMMENT**

➛ The shopping, or even window-shopping, is lots of fun here. Plan a 2-hour visit.

## *Living It Up*
# FREMONT STREET EXPERIENCE

**Fremont St. (between Main St. and Las Vegas Blvd.),**
**Las Vegas**
**(702) 678-5777**
**www.vegasexperience.com**

When the downtown area of Las Vegas (the original casino district) began to fade, city fathers came up with a solution that's the only one of its kind in the world. They created the Fremont Street Experience, a sound-and-light show that forms a canopy over four blocks of downtown and is enclosed as a pedestrian mall.

The Fremont Street Experience's 2.1 million lights and 540,000 watts of sound bring a variety of six-minute shows to the people watching. Kids delight seeing jets soar from one end of the canopy to the other; parents get into the Motown show and usually end up dancing. Adding to the experience are musicians and other street entertainers who perform regularly at various spots on the mall.

Occasionally, big-name bands are brought in—mostly rock bands of the '50s, '60s and '70s—to perform on stages at either end of the mall. Most of the time it's free, but a few times a year the mall is closed off for a performance by a truly big-name group and admission is charged.

Between the scheduled shows you can watch performance artists such as the Attitude Girls, view the outdoor Neon Museum (page 47), shop, grab something to eat or try your luck in the various casinos; the latter of course without the kids.

**SEASONS AND TIMES**

→ Year-round: Daily (on the hour), dusk—midnight. Shows change regularly, call for a current schedule.

**COST**

→ Free.

**GETTING THERE**

→ By car, take U.S. Hwy. 95 N. to Las Vegas Blvd. and head south. The Experience will be 2 blocks further. Pay parking on site, although you can get your parking ticket validated (for free parking) if you dine or gamble in one of the hotels. About 15 minutes from McCarran International Airport.

→ By public transit, take city bus route 301. It stops near the Fremont Street Experience parking garage.

**NEARBY**

→ Downtown casinos, Cashman Center & Field.

**COMMENT**

→ A misting system provides relief on hot days and there's heat for when it's cooler. Plan a 1-hour visit.

## *Live Long and Prosper*

# STAR TREK: THE EXPERIENCE

**Las Vegas Hilton, 3000 Paradise Rd., Las Vegas**
**(702) 732-5111**
**www.lv-hilton.com**

Attention, all Trekkies: boldly go where no one has gone before. Star Trek: The Experience at the Las Vegas Hilton is unique on this planet—or any planet for that matter.

Visitors to The Experience enter through the History of the Future Museum. It contains 200 items and is the largest permanent collection of *Star Trek* costumes and props in the world. It includes items from all nine *Star Trek* movies and the four TV series, complete with documentary labeling. There's weaponry, makeup, jewelry, character tableaux, film clips from everything *Star Trek*—all accompanied by a Vulcan soundtrack.

Everything is in glass cases, but the kids will not be bored. The real star of the show is the Voyage Through Space, a motion-simulator ride that lets visitors make a quick trip to the 24th century. Here, they get to enter the bridge of the USS *Enterprise* with Starfleet crewmembers (actors and animated characters) all around—and zip through distant galaxies in a desperate battle with the Klingons. Costumed interpreters stroll through the adjacent

Quark's Bar and Restaurant and Deep Space Nine Promenade.

All of this is a huge treat for serious Trekkies, and entertaining for anyone with even a passing *Star Trek* acquaintance. However, the Voyage Through Space and costumed interpreters may be a bit too intense for the littlest members of your crew.

**SEASONS AND TIMES**

➛ Year-round: Daily, 11 am—11 pm.

**COST**

➛ Individuals $19.95 ($16.95 for Nevada residents, but no price break for kids).

**GETTING THERE**

➛ By car, take I-15 N. to the Sahara Ave. E. Exit. Travel east on Sahara to Paradise Rd. and turn south. The Hilton's huge sign is impossible to miss. Free parking on site. About 20 minutes from McCarran International Airport.

➛ By public transit, take city bus route 108 to the Hilton.

**NEARBY**

➛ Las Vegas Convention Center, Sahara, Stratosphere.

**COMMENT**

➛ Elvis used to hang out at the Las Vegas Hilton—who really knows who is inside those *Star Trek* costumes? Plan a 2-hour visit. Serious Trekkies will want to stay longer.

## A New Outlook

# STRATOSPHERE HOTEL-CASINO

**2000 Las Vegas Blvd. S., Las Vegas**
**(702) 380-7777**
**www.stratlv.com**

Here is a chance to view the grandeur of Las Vegas all at one time—a 360-degree view from nearly 1,000 feet up.

The Stratosphere Hotel-Casino is a sleek landmark that dominates the Las Vegas skyline, no matter where you are. The casino is at the base of the tower with the hotel adjacent—but the real star of the show is the tower.

The Stratosphere's quiet, high-speed elevators take passengers to the indoor and outdoor observation decks on the 107th and 108th floors; not quite into the stratosphere, but close enough for most of us. The tallest building west of the Mississippi also boasts the tallest observation tower in the United States. At any time of the day—but especially at night, when the Las Vegas Valley looks like a bowl of glittering gems—the view is unmatched in the world. Perfect for newcomers, maps and descriptive panels will help you locate the sights, including casinos such as the Rio and Boulder Station.

Walking around on the observation deck is a thrill at any age and the multiple security fences make the outdoor deck safe for even the most adventurous child. The indoor deck is enclosed in glass that is canted to provide a view almost straight down.

Lunch and dinner are served in the Top of the Tower restaurant, where a revolving floor guarantees an ever-changing view. You'll find midway-type rides at the top of the tower and at the base (page 69).

**SEASONS AND TIMES**

➛ Year-round: Sun—Thu, 10 am—1 am; Fri—Sat, 10 am—2 am.

**COST**

➛ Adults $6, Nevada residents, senior citizens and children (4 to 12) $3, under 4 free.

**GETTING THERE**

➛ By car, take I-15 N. to Sahara Ave. E. Travel east on Sahara to Las Vegas Blvd. and turn north. The Stratosphere is 3 blocks further. Free parking on site. About 15 minutes from McCarran International Airport.

➛ By public transit, take city bus route 301. It stops along Las Vegas Blvd.

**NEARBY**

➛ The north end of the Strip, the Bonanza Gift Shop (world's largest).

**COMMENT**

➛ Anyone with even mild acrophobia might want to miss this one. A misting system provides relief on hot days and there's heat for when it's cooler. Plan a 1-hour visit.

## *Ahoy, Matey!*

# TREASURE ISLAND

**3300 Las Vegas Blvd. S., Las Vegas**
**(702) 894-7111**
**www.treasureislandlasvegas.com**

Just when you think you've been there, done that and seen everything that's clearly "only in Vegas"—there it is, a pirate battle performed by humans on full-sized ships. One of the ships sinks several times a night, weather permitting.

It's an age-old story and one to which kids gleefully relate. The pirates on their ship are gettin' a bit restless and Her Majesty's navy decides they'd better do something about it. The Queen's ship sails around a curve and into the harbor that separates Treasure Island from Las Vegas Boulevard. Guns fire; smoke fills the air. Pirates leap off their burning ship into the water as the English sailors seek similar refuge from their sinking vessel. (The men in the water are the reason the show doesn't go on if the weather is chilly or windy).

The boardwalk area in front of the show is tiered, but becomes sardine-packed during busy times. Those who are patient can watch the sunken ship rise again and head back around the curve to get ready for another show.

**SEASONS AND TIMES**

➛ Year-round (every 90 minutes weather permitting): Sun–Thu, 4 pm–10 pm; Fri–Sat, 4 pm–11:30 pm.

**COST**

➛ Free.

**GETTING THERE**

➛ By car, take I-15 N. to the Spring Mountain Rd. E. Exit. Travel east on Spring Mountain to Las Vegas Blvd. and turn south. Free parking on site. About 20 minutes from McCarran International Airport.

➛ By public transit, take city bus route 301. It stops along Las Vegas Blvd.

**NEARBY**

➛ Venetian, Mirage.

**COMMENT**

➛ Get there early for the best view, people line up well before a show. Plan a 45-minute visit.

## *Something's Erupting*
## VOLCANO

**Mirage, 3400 Las Vegas Blvd. S., Las Vegas**
**(702) 791-7111**
**www.mirage.com**

It starts with a blinking light, escalates into a low rumble and before you know it, flames erupt; then there's lava, tumbling down the hill right before your eyes.

It's not real lava, but that just makes the experience all the more enjoyable. Parents don't have to worry about their tots getting their tootsies toasted!

The volcano in front of the Mirage was the first big-scale free attraction for Las Vegas. Since it started belching in 1989, a parade of similar attractions has followed—the Strip will never be the same again.

The Mirage's volcanic mountain is attractive in the daytime, when it masquerades as a peaceful waterfall in a tranquil pond. It's only after dark—when the special-effects lava show is at its most dramatic—that the volcano comes to life.

Viewing occurs along the sidewalk between the volcano and Las Vegas Boulevard (the Strip). Because the show goes off so often and because it's the granddaddy of the G-rated shows, there's plenty of room for watching.

**SEASONS AND TIMES**

→ Year-round: Daily (every 15 minutes), dusk—midnight.

**COST**

→ Free.

**GETTING THERE**

→ By car, take I-15 N. to the Flamingo Rd. E. Exit. Travel east on Flamingo to Las Vegas Blvd. and turn north. The Mirage is right after Caesars Palace. Free parking on site. About 15 minutes from McCarran International Airport.

→ By public transit, take city bus route 301. It stops along Las Vegas Blvd.

**NEARBY**

→ Treasure Island, Caesars Palace, Venetian, Harrah's.

**COMMENT**

→ This Strip veteran still entertains nicely. The 15-minute show is a great complement to a gondola ride at The Venetian, or shopping at the Forum Shops at Caesars Palace.

# *Waters that Waltz*
# WATER SHOW

**Bellagio, 3600 Las Vegas Blvd. S., Las Vegas**
**(702) 693-7111**
**www.bellagiolasvegas.com**

Bellagio means "beautiful lake" in Italian, and that perfectly describes the 12-acre man-made lake in front of this resort.

The lake is lovely to look at, but in the afternoons and evenings, magic rises from it in the form of an elaborate sound, music and light show. More than 1,000 fountains shoot water up to 240 feet into the sky as the sound system plays everything from Aaron Copland to Luciano Pavarotti to Frank Sinatra.

Kids in particular, but adults, too, find the show enthralling as they watch the water sway, leap and spout in time to the music. It is not unusual to see tour buses stop at traffic signals along Las Vegas Boulevard (the Strip) and open their doors so passengers can take in the lovely sights and sounds.

There's plenty of free standing room on the sidewalk between the Strip and the Bellagio, making it a great stop for families. But be advised: children younger than 18 are not permitted inside the Bellagio unless they are hotel guests. Security officers are not shy about asking to see hotel keys. Certain allowances do apply, permitting admission to children between 5 and 18 who are having dinner or attending events at the hotel.

**SEASONS AND TIMES**

➛ Year-round: Every half-hour, Mon—Fri, 3 pm—8 pm; Sat—Sun, noon—8 pm. Every 15 minutes, daily, 8 pm—midnight.

**COST**

➛ Free.

**GETTING THERE**

➛ By car, take I-15 N. to the Flamingo Rd. E. Exit. Travel east on Flamingo to Las Vegas Blvd. and turn south. Free parking on site. About 10 minutes from McCarran International Airport.

➛ By public transit, take city bus route 301. It stops along Las Vegas Blvd.

**NEARBY**

➛ Aladdin, Paris, Bally's, Forum Shops at Caesars Palace.

**COMMENT**

➛ Great during the day, even better after dark. The 15-minute show is a great complement to a trip up the Eiffel Tower at Paris; or shopping at the Forum Shops at Caesars Palace or Desert Passage at the Aladdin.

## *Slaying the Dragon*
# DRAGON SHOW

Combine w/ King Arthur?

**Excalibur, 3850 Las Vegas Blvd. S., Las Vegas**
**(702) 597-7700**

Among the slick shows on the Strip, this one is a bit of a throwback, but that just adds to its charm.

The dragon battle on the north end of Excalibur starts with a truly impressive dragon moving up out of its lair to linger outside the cabin of the magician Merlin. The dragon breathes fire which is especially impressive to the smaller set—the same ones who don't seem to notice his slightly creaky movements.

As the dragon lurks, Merlin comes out of his cabin and rolls onto the pier to chase the beast away. It's a protracted battle—but Merlin wins in the end.

The battle can be viewed from two spots on the Tropicana Boulevard end of the resort; on ground-level sidewalks that border the moat and on the pedestrian bridge that stretches across Tropicana to connect Excalibur with New York-New York to the north. Get there early; viewing space is somewhat limited and curious crowds gather to see the show that is not as well-known as others on the Strip. After the show, you might want to head to the arcade or roller coaster at New York-New York (page 74).

**SEASONS AND TIMES**

→ Year-round (weather permitting): Daily (on the hour), dusk–midnight.

**COST**

→ Free.

**GETTING THERE**

→ By car, take I-15 N. to Tropicana Blvd. E. Travel east on Tropicana to Las Vegas Blvd. and turn south. Free parking on site. About 10 minutes from McCarran International Airport.

→ By public transit, take city bus route 301. It stops along Las Vegas Blvd.

**NEARBY**

→ Tropicana, MGM Grand, New York-New York, Mandalay Bay.

**COMMENT**

→ Especially of interest to younger kids. Plan a 30-minute visit.

CHAPTER 2

# MUSEUMS

# *Introduction*

In a city like Las Vegas—famous for its Elvis impersonators, bargain buffets and gaudy lights—you would expect to find places like the Neon Museum, Guinness World of Records Museum, Elvis-a-Rama Museum and Liberace Museum.

However, this is a community of 1.3 million people who have lives far more normal than the average tourist might suspect and this is reflected in the area's other museums. Kids—and their families—can easily spend a whole day creating music, "flying" a space shuttle and more at the hands-on Lied Discovery Children's Museum. For a lesson about the region's past, visit the Clark County Heritage Museum or the Boulder City-Hoover Dam Museum. Both are excellent historical museums and have lots of displays for touching. Kids will get a glimpse of ancient history in a far-off land at the Tomb and Museum of King Tutankhamun. You get a feel for what life is like elsewhere in the world at the Las Vegas Natural History Museum. It has stuffed and live animals, walk-through exhibits, animated dinosaurs and more.

For that elusive cultural experience, the Las Vegas Art Museum, with its permanent Dalis and varied traveling exhibits, completes the picture.

# *A Dam's History Comes Alive*
# BOULDER CITY-HOOVER DAM MUSEUM

**Boulder Dam Hotel, 1305 Arizona St., Boulder City**
**(702) 294-1988**

If the Tut Museum (page 49) reflects history of a civilization far away and long ago, its opposite is the Boulder City-Hoover Dam Museum, whose displays recount local history that took place just 70 years ago.

It was at the time of the Great Depression that the construction of the dam commenced—a project that would make life better for those who worked on it and for future generations. Visitors enter to displays explaining the Depression, the dust bowl and the devastation they brought. Throughout the museum, living-history audio-tapes play on a rotating basis and give witness testimony on various topics, from the primitive living conditions in the area to labor relations on the dam.

There is information on the importance of the dam project to the area's economy, and you can see a re-creation of its construction—how it was carved out of the canyon and what a massive undertaking it was to build. The dam had to be strong enough to hold back the mighty Colorado River.

There are lots of hands-on opportunities, too—doors to open, lids to pick up, even neighborhood gossip to eavesdrop on via telephone. What kid would not love trying to position a cement bucket for dumping? Adding to the fun, visitors are given a pass to be embossed at various posts in the museum. It makes a nice souvenir for children to have of their visit.

**SEASONS AND TIMES**

→ Year-round: Mon—Sat, 10 am—5 pm; Sun, noon—5 pm.

**COST**

→ Adults $2, seniors and students $1.

**GETTING THERE**

→ By car, take I-515 and U.S. Hwy. 93 S. to Boulder City, skip the bypass and follow the Nevada Hwy. into town. Shortly after the 93 fork, turn east onto Wyoming St. and then north onto Arizona St. The hotel is on the east side of the street. Free parking on site. About 45 minutes from McCarran International Airport.

→ By public transit, take city bus route 107 to Racetrack Rd. Transfer to route 116 to Boulder City.

**NEARBY**

→ Hoover Dam, Lake Mead National Recreation Area.

**COMMENT**

→ Plan at least a 1-hour visit to allow the kids plenty of time for touching.

# *Explore Nevada's Heritage at* THE CLARK COUNTY HERITAGE MUSEUM

**1830 S. Boulder Hwy., Henderson**
**(702) 455-7955**
**www.co.clark.nv.us/PARKREC/heritage.htm**

Everyone—children and grown-ups alike—can glimpse life in Las Vegas before the concrete-canyon casinos came to town by visiting the Clark County Heritage Museum in Henderson.

The museum building has a series of top-notch indoor tableaux showing how things were in the valley long ago, and not so long ago. Motion detectors bring each exhibit to life as people pass by. In one, they see and hear a dire wolf, a native species now extinct. In another, there is a model of the springs from which the city got its name. Displays depicting the lives of native people—notably Anasazi and Paiute—bring home the stark contrast of life in the valley today. Along the way, there is plenty for kids to explore in exhibits marked "please touch," such as a woven rabbit-fur robe, a cattle brand, a butter mold and a bar of lye soap.

Things only get better outdoors. Until recently, the museum grounds were surrounded by open desert. Today there are subdivisions, but they do little to detract from the loop nature trail. The train station has freight cars and a caboose that visitors can climb aboard and inspect. There's a ghost town with authentic period buildings that once served as a Strip tourist attraction. But the real star of the show may be the seven buildings, including five fully furnished homes from various periods, situated on a shady street. Through them, old Nevada lives again.

**SEASONS AND TIMES**

→ Year-round: Daily, 9 am—4:30 pm. Closed Christmas and New Year's.

**COST**

→ Adults $1.50, seniors (over 55) and youths (3 to 15) $1.

**GETTING THERE**

→ By car, take I-515 S. to the Lake Mead Dr. Exit and turn east. Turn south at Boulder Hwy. Continue to the museum, located on the east side of the street. Free parking on site. About 25 minutes from McCarran International Airport.

→ By public transit, take city bus route 107.

**NEARBY**

→ Boulder City, downtown Henderson.

**COMMENT**

→ Attend on a fair-weather day and plan a 2-hour visit.

## *Long Live the King*
# ELVIS-A-RAMA MUSEUM

**3401 Industrial Rd., Las Vegas**
**(702) 309-7200**
**www.elvisarama.com**

Who said Elvis has left the building? When visitors are welcomed to the Elvis-a-Rama Museum & Gift Shop, it's not by one of the Flying Elvi or another of Las Vegas' multitude of Elvis impersonators, but by the king himself. It seems a little spooky at first, but once his voice fades, visitors pass into a wonderland of all things Elvis.

There is Elvis' purple Lincoln, and his Cadillac limousine. There are costumes, awards and records. The most poignant displays pertain to Elvis' private life: letters he wrote, an Army inventory list of his possessions upon his return from Germany, his Army uniform, jewelry and pictures of his family. Along the way, signs explain about Elvis—especially his penchant for giving gifts. A few times each day, an Elvis impersonator performs on the museum's little stage to bring back a reminder of the King.

Some of this may be a little dull for kids unfamiliar with the Presley legend. However, an explanation from Mom or Dad—which will be easy if they are Elvis fans—should clear things up. And most children will be dazzled by the colors.

**SEASONS AND TIMES**
➛ Year-round: Daily, 10 am–6 pm.

**COST**
➛ $9.95 per person, under 13 free.

**GETTING THERE**
➛ By car, take I-15 N. to Spring Mountain Rd. Travel east on Spring Mountain to Fashion Show Dr. Turn north on Fashion Show to Industrial. Continue north on Industrial to the museum. It will be on the west side of the street. Free parking on site. About 20 minutes from McCarran International Airport.
➛ By public transit, take city bus route 105.

**NEARBY**
➛ Fashion Show Mall, the Stardust, the New Frontier.

**COMMENT**
➛ You may want to give the kids a little Elvis background beforehand. Plan a 1-hour visit.

*History by the Book*

# GUINNESS WORLD OF RECORDS MUSEUM

**2780 Las Vegas Blvd. S., Las Vegas**
**(702) 792-0640**
**www.lasvegas.com/lv/guinness**

The Guinness World of Records Museum may sound like the quintessential tourist trap, but it is surprisingly entertaining for adults and kids get a kick out of the extremes. For example, the museum has models of the world's tallest man and the shortest woman, as well as the oldest man and the person with the longest neck. Live-action films add to the entertainment. One screen shows clip after clip of elaborate domino setups around the world with the little blocks arranged to fall in intricate, colorful patterns (and sometimes in amazingly long paths). There are films showcasing all sorts of human feats, some admirable and others not, such as the woman who holds the record for the distance she can make her eyes bulge out from her face.

Sports, movie and music feats are also celebrated, but it seems that oddity does reign supreme. You won't find any hands-on displays in the museum; however, if you want to learn about the guy who holds the record for spending time in a tub with the most rattlesnakes, this museum is for you.

**SEASONS AND TIMES**

➛ Summer (June–Aug): Daily, 9 am–8 pm. Winter (Sept–May): Daily, 9 am–6 pm.

**COST**

➛ Adults $4.95, seniors, students and members of the military $3.95, children (under 13) $2.95.

**GETTING THERE**

➛ By car, take I-15 N. to Sahara Ave. E. Travel east on Sahara to Las Vegas Blvd. S. and turn south. Continue to the museum. It's located on the west side of the street. Free parking on site. About 25 minutes from McCarran International Airport.

➛ By public transit, take city bus route 301.

**NEARBY**

➛ The Sahara, Circus Circus, Adventuredome, Wet 'n Wild.

**COMMENT**

➛ Plan a 1-hour visit.

## *The Art is the Draw*
# THE LAS VEGAS ART MUSEUM

**9600 W. Sahara Ave., Las Vegas**
**(702) 360-8000**
**www.lastplace.com/EXHIBITS/LVAM**

The Las Vegas Art Museum is a big, airy, stunning building. It hosts traveling exhibits as well as a small, permanent collection.

The building itself is new—constructed as part of the Las Vegas-Clark County Library District and opened in 1997. Its roots go back to 1950, when the Las Vegas Art League was founded by a group of female plein-air desert painters who were newcomers to the valley.

The museum has two Salvador Dali works on permanent loan—the controversial *Vision of Hell*, a 1962 work commissioned by the Blue Army of Our Lady of Fatima; and *Lune a la Calanzyne de Culis*, painted when he was 10. Temporary exhibitions have included such shows as Three California Painters, showcasing works by Denise Bankuti, Neil Doty and Herb Tannen; and Art Beyond Borders, highlighting art from 40 countries around the world.

A sculpture garden that's part of the museum's plan for the future certainly would be of interest to young children, as well as art lovers of all ages. In the meantime, young visitors will have to make do with what is on hand. That should not be much of a problem though, since many of the large works have attention-grabbing bright colors.

Occasional museum workshop classes are offered for all ages, and a school of digital art is being planned. If the kids get bored, promise them a visit to the library next door.

**SEASONS AND TIMES**

→ Year-round: Tue—Sat, 10 am—5 pm; Sun, 1 pm—5 pm.

**COST**

→ Adults $3, seniors $2, students with Nevada ID $1.

**GETTING THERE**

→ By car, take I-15 N. to Sahara Ave. W. Travel west on Sahara. The museum is located on the north side of the street. Free parking on site. About 40 minutes from McCarran International Airport.

→ By public transit, take city bus route 204.

**NEARBY**

→ Desert Breeze Park.

**COMMENT**

→ This is a great place for kids to learn to appreciate art. Plan a 1-hour visit.

*Sharks in the Desert!*

# LAS VEGAS NATURAL HISTORY MUSEUM

**900 Las Vegas Blvd. N., Las Vegas**
**(702) 384-DINO (3466)**
**www.vegaswebworld.com/lvnathistory**

A visit to the Las Vegas Natural History Museum reveals how the museum has evolved over the years. Its International Wildlife Room, billed as showcasing "mammals from around the world," is an older-style, static exhibit—basically a large open area filled with stuffed mammals.

Far better and of greater interest to younger visitors are the museum's newer exhibits. The Marine Life Room has models of sharks and other sea creatures, plus a large tank that is home to various live sharks. The Dinosaur Den boasts animated dinosaurs including a few that are not commonly seen.

Better still is the Wild Nevada Room, whose wonderfully detailed tableaux recreate the sights, sounds—even smells—of the various desert environments. Explore Africa features a savanna display and a spectacular, highly detailed rain forest exhibit. Visitors can push buttons to highlight particulars of the rain forest and hear explanations of their ecological roles.

If this fails to fascinate the little ones, take them past the two 14-foot-long snakes in the Python Pit.

**SEASONS AND TIMES**

➛ Year-round: Daily, 9 am—4 pm. Closed Christmas.

**COST**

➛ Adults $5.50, seniors, members of the military and students $4.50, children (4 to 12) $3, under 4 free.

**GETTING THERE**

➛ By car, take I-15 N. to Sahara Ave. E. Travel east on Sahara to Las Vegas Blvd. and turn north. Continue north on Las Vegas, past downtown to the museum. It's located on the east side of the street. Free parking on site. About 25 minutes from McCarran International Airport.

➛ By public transit, take city bus route 401.

**NEARBY**

➛ The Lied Discovery Children's Museum, Cashman Center, Cashman Field.

**COMMENT**

➛ Plan a 2-hour visit.

## *A Glittering Display*
# THE LIBERACE MUSEUM

**1775 E. Tropicana Ave., Las Vegas**
**(702) 798-5595**
**www.liberace.org**

Dazzling: nobody could do it like Liberace. His sparkling legacy lives on in the two-building museum dedicated to this consummate showman.

The museum may baffle young children, even more than the Elvis-a-Rama (page 37). After all, Liberace's heyday is a distant memory even for a lot of baby boomers. Still, it is worth the stop to look at the ultimate camp icon.

Through pictures, words and displays of his personal possessions, visitors see and learn about Liberace in his early years, before the pianist became the showman. Among the exhibits is his gold lamé dinner jacket, whose sparkling debut in 1955 would be the mother of all rhinestone-studded spectaculars to come—even Liberace called them "an expensive joke." If he had continued to wear a simple tuxedo or tails, there probably would be no museum for people to visit today.

Liberace had a way of taking inspiration from a single item. The platinum candelabra, a gift from Bill Harrah of Harrah's Reno that started the ball rolling, is here. You can also see his diamond grand-piano ring and the diamond-on-diamond buttons that each bear a letter spelling out Liberace's name. Add a rhinestone car, a desk that once belonged to Czar Nicholas and Liberace's hot pants outfit from the 100th anniversary of the Statue of Liberty, and you have an entertaining collection.

**SEASONS AND TIMES**

➛ Year-round: Mon–Sat, 10 am–5 pm; Sun, 1 pm–5 pm.

**COST**

➛ Adults $6.95, seniors and students $4.95, children (under 13) free when accompanied by an adult.

**GETTING THERE**

➛ By car, take I-15 N. to Tropicana Ave. E. Travel east on Tropicana. The museum is located on the south side of the street. Free parking on site. About 10 minutes from McCarran International Airport.

➛ By public transit, take city bus route 201.

**NEARBY**

➛ Sunset Park, Thomas & Mack Center of the University of Nevada-Las Vegas.

**COMMENT**

➛ Give the kids some Liberace background beforehand. Plan a 1-hour visit.

*Busy Bodies*

# LIED DISCOVERY CHILDREN'S MUSEUM

**833 Las Vegas Blvd. N., Las Vegas**
**(702) 382-5437**
**www.ldcm.org**

Las Vegas may be a playground for grown-ups, but who said they should have all the fun? The Lied Discovery Children's Museum offers kids all kinds of hands-on enjoyment and opportunities for learning.

Just past the museum entrance gate, a large, ornate dollhouse—its walls opened wide to reveal the meticulous detail within—gets things off to an arty start. But the museum has plenty of science-oriented exhibits too, as well as those dedicated to communication and consumer science.

In the shopping exhibit, kids can push shopping carts past grocery shelves, select items and compare prices, and take their "purchases" to the cash register and ring them up. Elsewhere, they can see how sound travels by talking into a special tube or get an inside peek at the workings of a periscope. A harmless-looking room with a diamond pattern on the floor turns out to be a real challenge—even for the most coordinated. The optical illusion conceals a floor that slopes sharply.

Everyone can experience the thrill of a space shuttle mission in the museum's re-created cockpit. Don't forget to check out the karaoke-style radio station or the musical floor; kids love hopping on the blocks to play a song. A steel drum with diagrams enables them to create their own music.

Add the standard kids'-museum stuff such as static globes and tricky mirrors and your youngsters will be happy for hours.

**SEASONS AND TIMES**

→ Year-round: Tue—Sun, 10 am—5 pm. Open Mondays on school holidays.

**COST**

→ Adults $5, seniors, members of the military, students with ID and youths (2 to 17) $4.

**GETTING THERE**

→ By car, take I-15 N. to Sahara Ave. E. Travel east on Sahara to Las Vegas Blvd. S. and turn north. Continue on to Las Vegas Blvd. N. and the museum. It will be on the west side of the street. Free parking on site. About 35 minutes from McCarran International Airport.

→ By public transit, take city bus route 401.

**NEARBY**

→ The Las Vegas Natural History Museum, the Las Vegas Library, Cashman Center, Cashman Field.

**COMMENT**

→ Plan a 2-hour visit.

# *Getting that Las Vegas Glow*
# THE NEON MUSEUM

**Fremont Street Experience Pedestrian Mall (Fremont and adjoining streets), Las Vegas**
**(702) 229-5366**

Las Vegas is known for its neon signs and its desert climate. This means that old signs don't rust, they just keep on glowing. So when local preservationists decided that the city's old commercial signs should be saved, and the biggest electric sign company's boneyard was full, the Neon Museum was born.

The museum, which is outdoors on the pedestrian mall of the Fremont Street Experience (page 18), has a small but growing collection. It contains the colorful, large horse-and-rider sign from the old Hacienda Hotel and a small but quaintly interesting sign for the Chief Hotel Court dated 1940, with a notation "steamed heat" and an arrow pointing the way. Then there is the 1961 sign from the Flame Restaurant, once on Desert Inn Road, that still promises meals served 24 hours a day, although the restaurant has been closed for years. The martini glass sign from the former Red Barn, also from the 1960s, rises out of the sidewalk à la Leaning Tower of Pisa.

Kids will no doubt be tickled to see the huge Andy Anderson neon sign from 1956, the old mascot of Anderson Dairy. There is also the non-neon but still-interesting 1966 lighted sign from the old Aladdin Hotel—a big Aladdin-style lamp studded with golden incandescent bulbs.

The signs are in several areas of the five-block Fremont Street Experience pedestrian mall, including several on the Third Street expansion area. Others are flanked on one side by the construction site for Neonopolis, the city's downtown redevelopment project, and on the other side by the elaborate neon of Race Rock, a large restaurant brimming with racing memorabilia.

The city recently acquired additional property close to the current Neon Museum. Many of the signs housed in the sign company's two-acre storage yard will be relocated to the new site.

**SEASONS AND TIMES**

➛ Year round: Daily, 24 hours a day.

**COST**

➛ Free.

**GETTING THERE**

➛ By car, take I-15 N. to Sahara Ave. E. Head east on Sahara to Las Vegas Blvd. and turn north. Follow Las Vegas until you reach Fremont Street Experience. Parking is available in the FSE parking garage or nearby hotel garages. About 30 minutes from McCarran International Airport.

➛ By public transit, take city bus route 301.

**NEARBY**

➛ Fremont Street Experience, Lied Discovery Children's Museum, Las Vegas Natural History Museum.

**COMMENT**

➛ A misting system provides relief on hot days. For cooler weather, there is outdoor heat. Best viewed after dark. Combine your visit with the sights and sounds of the Fremont Street Experience. Plan a 2-hour visit.

*Tut-tut, King Tut*

# THE TOMB AND MUSEUM OF KING TUTANKHAMUN

**Luxor, 3900 Las Vegas Blvd. S., Las Vegas**
**(702) 262-4000**
**www.luxor.com**

Here is an only-in-Las Vegas attraction: a full-size reproduction of the tomb of King Tutankhamun—affectionately known as "King Tut."

This hotel-casino is unique; it is the Egyptian-themed Luxor and is complete with Sphinx and pyramid-shaped main building. Inside, hotel rooms are reached by "inclinators" instead of elevators.

But back to the exhibit. Students of archeology may recall that Tut's tomb was discovered in 1922. When asked what was inside, its discoverer replied "wonderful things!" The Las Vegas version is also filled with wonderful things. It includes a copy of

Tut's gold-topped sarcophagus tomb and other articles created by artisans using the same materials as the 3,300-year-old originals. The items are positioned as they were in the actual tomb. A 15-minute audiotape tour explains it all.

Whether or not they know Tut from their toenails, children will no doubt be amazed at such dazzling bits of re-created antiquity.

**SEASONS AND TIMES**

→ Year-round: Sun—Thu, 9 am—11 pm; Fri—Sat, 9 am—1 am.

**COST**

→ $5 per person.

**GETTING THERE**

→ By car, take I-15 N. to Tropicana Ave. E. Take Tropicana east to Las Vegas Blvd. and head south to the Luxor. It's located on the west side of the street. Free parking on site. About 10 minutes from McCarran International Airport.

→ By public transit, take city bus route 301.

**NEARBY**

→ Mandalay Bay, New York-New York, the MGM Grand.

**COMMENT**

→ You may want to combine this stop with a visit to the Dragon Battle at the Excalibur, a ride on the roller coaster at New York-New York or a walk through the Lion Habitat at the MGM Grand. Plan a 30-minute visit.

CHAPTER 3

# IN YOUR NEIGHBORHOOD

# *Introduction*

Las Vegas is one of the world's leading entertainment capitals. While there's much for families to do on the Strip—entertainment's epicenter—the traffic and non-family offerings can sometimes be a bit much. Don't worry. The neighborhoods in this metropolitan area of 1.3 million people offer plenty of family-friendly activities and most cost little or nothing at all. Take the kids bowling, skating or to a family amusement center. Visit a library, craft store or farmer's market, or let them create their own teddy bears. Whatever your interest—or that of your children—there's plenty to do, right in your own backyard.

# *Strike Out for Fun*
# BOWLING ALLEYS

Bowling? You want bowling? If Las Vegas isn't the bowling capital of America, it comes pretty darn close. The game is big and like most businesses, many bowling alleys are open 24 hours a day.

Bowling is an ideal outing for children of all ages, as well as their parents. Toddlers enjoy rolling the ball, even if they play by their own rules. More than just fun—it's inexpensive. A whole family can play a few games for under $20 (including shoe rentals). Alleys throughout Las Vegas cater to families; a few are listed below. Even the bowling centers in the casinos—where many of the largest are located—are quite friendly to kids. Lightweight balls are available, as are gutter bumpers.

You don't have to call ahead to arrange for bumpers. Just show up and the staff will set them up, although a limited number are available and it's first-come, first-serve.

You should call ahead however, to check on lane availability. Las Vegas is a big bowling league town and many centers are fully booked at seemingly unlikely times. To avoid disappointment, call the center of choice and make the pertinent inquiries.

One other note: many of the centers (especially casino-based centers) offer child-care facilities. So if your family includes a tot who's too little to heft even the lightest ball, there's a spot where he or she can have fun, too.

**BOULDER BOWL**
**504 California Ave., Boulder City (702) 293-2368**
**Birthday parties, kids' leagues, no bumpers.**

**GOLD COAST HOTEL & CASINO**
**4000 W. Flamingo Rd., Las Vegas (702) 367-4700**
**Birthday parties, kids' leagues, automated bumpers.**

**MAHONEY'S SILVER NUGGET**
**2140 N. Las Vegas Blvd., Las Vegas**
**(702) 320-BOWL (2695)**
**Birthday parties, bumpers, kids' leagues including bike leagues. Cosmic Bowling at designated times.**

**SUNCOAST HOTEL & CASINO**
**9090 Alta Dr., Las Vegas (702) 636-7400**
**Birthday parties, automated bumpers, kids' leagues.**

**SUNSET LANES**
**4451 E. Sunset Rd., Henderson (702) 736-2695**
**Birthday parties, kids' leagues, bumpers.**

*Check it out*

# CHILDREN'S LIBRARIES

Visiting a public library may be a great way to escape the blistering heat of a Las Vegas summer day, but there's so much more—especially if you want to help your kids build a lifetime reading habit.

The Las Vegas/Clark County Library District has 12 urban libraries, plus 11 in rural or outlying areas. All offer free library cards for kids (with parental permission if they're under 14) and children's sections. The rural branches vary in the services they offer (depending on the size of the library and the community), but any urban branch is a child's paradise.

In addition to children's literature, from picture to reference books to popular periodicals, larger branches also feature outstanding programs.

These include crafts series (with kids making something different to take home each week), puppet shows, peace celebrations and authors' birthday celebrations that help young readers learn about that person's works. Children can attend teddy bear teas with teddy bear parades and movie showings complete with popcorn. There are jungle-theme programs and special events around the holidays (including a Chinese New Year celebration). The libraries' song-and-story series is popular, as are individual story times for lap-sitters, pre-schoolers, school-age kids and the whole family. To learn more, stop in or call any local library. Contact the main branch at (702) 382-7919, or visit the district's website at www.lvccld.lib.nv.us/index.htm

## *Beads, Boxes and Things*
# CRAFTY PLACES

Here's an opportunity to drag the kids away from the video games and TV reruns. Take them to a craft store, load up on supplies and spend the weekend creating.

Local craft shops have every craft you could imagine, and a few you probably couldn't. Especially big with kids these days are beaded-animal projects. They can make everything from key rings to pins to dresser-top doodads in the shape of their favorite animal.

Another good craft item is polymer clay, which can be molded into myriad shapes that become permanent when baked. Rubber stamping—especially with big chunky stamps that are easy for little hands to hold—offers a range of possibilities. You can even introduce your little ones to the world of scrapbooks.

Need some inspiration or instruction? Local craft stores, including outlets of national chains like Jo-Ann etc. and Michael's Arts & Crafts, offer classes for kids. Don't forget the museums. Workshops are scheduled periodically at the Lied Discovery Children's Museum (page 45). These include informal workshops where anyone can drop in and make a little something to take home. More structured workshops allow kids to create cup-and-string phones, Valentines, corncob prints and other projects.

**JO-ANN ETC.**
**2160 N. Rainbow Blvd., Las Vegas (702) 646-2334**
**3890 S. Maryland Pkwy., Las Vegas (702) 791-0900**

**LIED DISCOVERY CHILDREN'S MUSEUM**
**833 Las Vegas Blvd. N., Las Vegas (702) 382-3445**

**MICHAEL'S ARTS & CRAFTS**
**Multiple locations. Look in the telephone directory for the one nearest you.**

# *Choose Your Own Fun*
# FAMILY FUN CENTERS

Looking for some good old-fashioned family fun without straying far from your neighborhood? The amusement centers in Las Vegas provide it. They offer fewer big-time thrills than the monster-size amusements parks such as MGM Grand Adventure and Adventuredome at Circus Circus, but the centers still have a decent variety of activities that appeal to all ages.

At Mountasia, families find an indoor roller-skating rink (in-line skaters are welcome), 18 holes of miniature golf, bumper boats, go-carts and ubiquitous video games. Scandia Family Fun Center is even bigger—and has a view of the Las Vegas Strip—with three 18-hole miniature golf courses, 18 automated pitching machines (hardball and softball), bumper boats, Lil' Indy raceway and an arcade.

Pricing is flexible. Parents can choose to pay per activity or by the package. Party packages and group rates are available. Hours are tailored to various family members with afternoon and weekend morning hours for tots and younger kids, and weekend evening hours that appeal to teens. Mountasia has periodic Cosmic Night events for teens as well.

**MOUNTASIA**
**2050 Olympic Ave., Henderson (702) 454-4386**

**SCANDIA FAMILY FUN CENTER**
**2900 Sirius Ave., Las Vegas (702) 364-0070**

## *Skate the Day Away*
# ICE AND ROLLER RINKS

Whether your style is wheels or blades—or both—you'll find something for the whole family in the Las Vegas Valley. And the best thing is, the rinks are an all-weather proposition. You can roller skate when it's chilly outside and ice skate if it's hot.

All of the rinks welcome family groups and what better way to spend an afternoon than to help a young one find his or her skating legs. Parents may come away feeling that their arms are a little longer, but the family's guaranteed to have fun. And as the kids learn a new skill that'll last them a lifetime, they're also getting good exercise. Make sure they wear proper fitting headgear.

The rinks offer all of the accouterments you'd expect, such as birthday parties, snack bars, private lessons, classes, as well as youth and adult leagues for ice and roller hockey. All offer skate rentals and allow skaters to bring their own; roller rinks also permit in-line skates.

**CRYSTAL PALACE SKATING CENTER**
**4680 Boulder Hwy., Las Vegas (702) 458-7107**
**3901 N. Rancho Dr., Las Vegas (702) 645-4892**
**9295 W. Flamingo Ave., Las Vegas (702) 253-9832**

**LAS VEGAS ICE ARENA**
**7675 Sultana St., Las Vegas (702) 260-7465**

**LAS VEGAS ICE GARDEN**
**3896 Swenson St., Las Vegas (702) 731-1062**

**SAHARA ICE PALACE**
**800 Karen Ave., Las Vegas (702) 862-4262**

**SANTE FE STATION HOTEL & CASINO**
**4949 N. Rancho Dr., Las Vegas (702) 658-4991**

# *Places to* PAINT YOUR OWN POTTERY

Here's the ultimate gift for the grandparents; a mug, plate, bowl, candleholder—almost any type of ceramic piece you can imagine—decorated with permanent art created by their grandchildren. And think of the fun kids will have creating the pieces. You name it, your kids can paint it at one of the Las Vegas-area ceramic studios.

Most shops feature an array of already completed bisques (ceramic items) that simply need to be painted with non-toxic paint. The studio supplies the paint, brushes, stencils, sponges and tips to get your kids' creative juices flowing. Some establishments charge a flat fee for the bisques, which start at about $5, and an hourly fee for the painting. Younger children tend to finish their projects quickly, so it's a good idea to limit the number of items they can paint; otherwise this activity will become expensive. After the painting is done, the shop glazes and fires the piece. You can pick it up a few days later.

Some shops have special rates for kids and most are willing to arrange birthday parties where whole groups of little ones can put their creative skills to the test. This is a great family activity, too. While the kids are creating pieces for posterity, Mom and Dad will find an outlet for their own artistic bent, creating items that are both decorative and practical.

**ALL FIRED UP**
**2381 E. Windmill Pkwy., Las Vegas (702) 269-4444**

**THE ARTFUL POTTER**
**2351 N. Rainbow Blvd., Las Vegas (702) 638-1775**
**8826 S. Eastern Ave., Las Vegas (702) 966-6300**

**COLOR ME MINE**
**7541 W. Lake Mead Blvd., Las Vegas (702) 869-9709**

## *Cool Places to Play*
# SWIMMING POOLS

If the kids are looking to make a splash—or maybe just be cool—the Las Vegas Valley, where municipal swimming pools abound, is the place to be.

Clark County operates 13 outdoor pools—10 near the city and three in outlying areas. The City of Las Vegas has seven outdoor pools and one indoor. The City of Henderson offers residents five outdoor pools and two indoor, and the City of North Las Vegas operates three outdoor pools. Most offer swimming and water-orientation classes for tots as young as six months, as well as diving classes, lifeguard training, party accommodations and of course, free-swim hours.

More pools are planned. As new ones are built, they come with more bells and whistles than you'd expect from a community pool. The Whitney Ranch complex in Henderson, for example, has an indoor pool that's great for year-round training, lap swimming and lifeguard training. The outdoor pool, with a wade-in shallow end, has water-spraying equipment that makes it great summer fun for the smallest tot.

For more information about community pools, contact:

**CITY OF HENDERSON**
**(702) 565-4264 • www.cityofhenderson.com**

**CITY OF LAS VEGAS**
**(702) 229-6309 • www.ci.las-vegas.nv.us/aquatics.htm**

**CITY OF NORTH LAS VEGAS PARKS AND RECREATION DEPARTMENT**
**(702) 633-1171 • www.ci.north-las-vegas.nv.us**

**CLARK COUNTY PARKS AND RECREATION DEPARTMENT**
**(702) 455-8508 • www.co.clark.nv.us/PARKREC/Aquatics.htm**

*Create Your Own New Friend*

# TEDDY BEAR WORKSHOPS

Every kid loves teddy bears. There's something about the cute, cuddly, furry little guys that makes kids feel safe and secure. Usually teddies arrive with identities and personalities already created by the manufacturer. Enter the era of the create-it-yourself teddy bear. Until recently, making a bear by hand was a daunting project for all but the most experienced crafter—a process so drawn-out it was sure to lose a kid's attention.

All that's changed. The latest creative-expression craze is bear workshops, where kids and adults alike can create their own furry friends. In addition to bears, you can make your own cows, cats, dogs, monkeys, horses, pigs, frogs—you name it—in various sizes.

The shops provide the pre-sewn bear or other animal, which start at about $10. Kids get to stuff them and stitch them (this process is supervised and mechanized for ease), groom and dress them from a whole line of accessories. (There's an extra fee for accessories.) To completely outfit your new friend, bear dens and condos are available, too. The stores offer birthday parties—which doubles the fun with every party guest taking home their very own new friend!

**BUILD-A-BEAR WORKSHOP**
**Desert Passage, 3663 Las Vegas Blvd. S., Las Vegas**
**(702) 836-0899**

**STUFFY BEAR FACTORY**
**Boulevard Mall, 3680 Maryland Pkwy., Las Vegas**
**(702) 967-BEAR (2327)**

# Other Neighborhood Haunts

## Farmer's Markets

Looking for a nice salad for dinner tonight? Don't run to the supermarket for that too-ripe/not-ripe-enough trucked-in stuff. Stop by the farmer's market. Chances are good there's one right in your neighborhood—or at least close by. Besides freshness (typical spring offerings include such delights as red beefsteak tomatoes, tangelos, fresh olive oil and strawberries), the bonus is that kids will get an idea that some things really do grow on trees. There are plenty of non-produce offerings too, such as funnel cakes, kettle corn, European-style bread, Cajun-style foods, works by artists and more. For a rundown on farmer's markets around Las Vegas, see page 129 in this book.

CHAPTER 4

# PLACES TO PLAY

# *Introduction*

Many people think Las Vegas is a spot to stay inside and gamble, but the city offers plenty of opportunities for outdoor family fun. Ice-skating, swimming, plus more prosaic activities such as amusement parks, miniature golf and good old American baseball are available.

One thing to keep in mind—this is the desert, and temperatures on mid-summer afternoons can climb well above 100 degrees in the sun. So take your sunscreen, wear a hat and pack plenty of water.

# *Hooting and Hollering at the* ADVENTUREDOME

**Circus Circus, 2880 Las Vegas Blvd. S., Las Vegas**
**(702) 794-3939**
**www.circuscircus-lasvegas.com**

This is a rarity. The world's largest enclosed theme park, the one shown in the movie *Baby Geniuses*, offers five acres of spine-tingling fun and excitement. It is covered by a giant pink dome, so it's comfortable inside whether the mercury dips or soars as much as the rides.

And what rides they are! For the smaller set, there is an extensive variety in varying degrees of gentleness—the Road Runner, the mini-Himalayan and the Thunderbirds, where kids fly above the crowd in 1920 vintage airplanes. The Drifters is a hot-air-balloon-style Ferris wheel and Miner Mike features a tour along a track in miniature coal bins.

For more daring thrill-seekers, there's the Canyon Blaster double-loop, double-corkscrew roller coaster with an initial drop of 90 feet, moving at speeds of up to 55 miles per hour. The Rim Runner is a raft-style ride that floats passengers through scenic landscaping within the Adventuredome, before plunging down a 60-foot waterfall. Then there's the Inverter, offering 360 degrees of constant G-force. Adventuredome has clowns too, as well as games of chance, laser tag, miniature golf and lots of carnival-style food and merchandise booths.

Most of the attractions are included in a one-price pass, although tickets can be purchased separately. Extra charges apply for some rides.

**SEASONS AND TIMES**

➛ Year-round: Daily, 10 am—midnight.

**COST**

➛ Unlimited ride pass: $16.95 for those 48 inches and taller, $12.95 for those 33 to 48 inches tall. Children shorter than 33 inches are admitted free. Individual ride tickets range from $3 to $5.

**GETTING THERE**

➛ By car, take I-15 N. to the Sahara Ave. E. Exit. Travel east on Sahara to Las Vegas Blvd. and turn south. Circus Circus and Adventuredome will be the first big complex you see. Free parking on site. About 20 minutes from McCarran International Airport.

➛ By public transit, take city bus route 301. It stops along Las Vegas Blvd.

**NEARBY**

➛ Riviera, Stardust, Stratosphere.

**COMMENT**

➛ The site is big and with so many activities packed under one dome, it's crowded. It is a good idea to pick a time and place where you can meet should members of your family decide to strike out on their own. Lost children can be found at the security office. Plan a 3-hour visit.

# *Zoom with a View at the* HIGH ROLLER AND BIG SHOT

**Stratosphere Hotel-Casino,**
**2000 Las Vegas Blvd. S., Las Vegas**
**(702) 380-7777**
**www.stratlv.com**

If simply looking down at Las Vegas from 1,000 feet in the Stratosphere's tower (page 22) isn't exciting enough, how about riding the roller coaster or boomerang ride at that height? The High Roller coaster and the Big Shot are located atop the Stratosphere Hotel-Casino in the center of Las Vegas.

It's true that the High Roller is a tame coaster, but at this height, who's complaining? Passengers scream expectantly as the cars near the first hill, only to find it is a gentle dip. The coaster, whose tracks are tilted slightly toward the tower, moves slowly enough as it circles the tower twice to provide a breath-taking 360-degree view of the Las Vegas Valley. Once the initial apprehension wears off, it's a great ride. Passengers strapped into the Big Shot get hurled to the top—bungee-style. At night they see nothing but black sky and stars, during the day nothing but blue!

These two rides were definitely not designed for tots. The Stratosphere developed the Stratofair, an area near the base of the tower with carnival games for families and rides for small fry. The Little Shot is an adorable replica of its big brother above—even at this slightly elevated height there is a good view for the faint of heart. Other rides include the Sky Wheel Ferris wheel and the Hover Crash bumper cars.

**SEASONS AND TIMES**

➛ Year-round (weather permitting): Sun—Thu, 10 am—1 am; Fri—Sat, 10 am—2 am.

**COST**

➛ Rides: Big Shot $8, High Roller $5, Little Shot, Sky Wheel and Hover Crash $3 each. Tower: Adults $6, Nevada residents, senior citizens and children (4 to 12) $3, under 4 free. Value-added tower and ride passes available. Also repeat-ride discounts.

**GETTING THERE**

➛ By car, take I-15 N. to the Sahara Ave. E. Exit. Travel east on Sahara to Las Vegas Blvd. and turn north. The Stratosphere is 3 blocks further. Free parking on site. About 20 minutes from McCarran International Airport.

➛ By public transit, take city bus route 301. It stops along Las Vegas Blvd.

**NEARBY**

➛ Sahara, Bonanza Gift Shop (world's largest).

**COMMENT**

➛ A great alternative for the smaller set. The misting system is near the outdoor kiddie rides for hot summer days. Plan a 2-hour visit.

# *Head for the Hills*
# INDOOR CLIMBING GYMS

Want to give your kids a place to climb to their heart's content and not worry they are going to get hurt? Rock-climbing walls may be the answer.

There are a number of climbing walls in the Las Vegas area, although some, such as those in spas, are not accessible to kids. The better choice is to take them to a multi-use activity center. Once they tire of the rock wall, they can ride the go-carts, play miniature golf or try the virtual-reality games.

Most gyms allow even tots to climb, provided a parent or guardian is with them. Many offer birthday parties. Climbing rates start at about $7; multi-use facilities offer package prices.

**ALL-AMERICAN SPORTPARK**
**121 E. Sunset Rd., Las Vegas**
**(702) 317-7777**

**GAMEWORKS**
**Showcase Mall, 3785 Las Vegas Blvd. S., Las Vegas**
**(702) 432-4263**

**POWERHOUSE INDOOR CLIMBING CENTER**
**8201 W. Charleston Blvd., Las Vegas**
**(702) 254-5604**

**VEGAS ROCK GYM**
**3065 E. Patrick Lane, Las Vegas**
**(702) 434-3388**

# *Life's a Beach at* LAKE MEAD NATIONAL RECREATION AREA

**601 Nevada Hwy., Boulder City**
**(702) 293-8906**
**www.nps.gov/lame**

Beaches in the middle of the desert? Yep—they abound at Lake Mead National Recreation Area, southeast of Las Vegas. The area is actually made up of Lake Mead (formed by the construction of Hoover Dam in the 1930s), and the smaller Lake Mohave, which offer beaches, marinas and coves that provide access to swimmers. Sandy Beach is here, the largest sand beach near Las Vegas.

The recreational areas are busy year-round, but most of the swimming takes place in the summer when the temperature of the clean, clear water can stretch up into the 80s. Beware, though; Lake Mead isn't a naturally occurring body of water. It was formed when Black Canyon was dammed, hence the canyon walls are steep. For that reason, drop-offs are common. There are no lifeguards. Don't expect changing rooms, although you can change in the restrooms.

Lake Mead is a big destination for boaters. Swimmers have to be cautious lest a boat wanders too near. If you're a boater, there are a number of marinas for access and boat rentals are available.

Lake Mead has other attractions for families. You can read about them on page 148.

**SEASONS AND TIMES**

➛ Park: Year-round, daily, 24 hours a day. Visitors center: Daily, 8:30 am—4:30 pm. Closed Thanksgiving, Christmas and New Year's.

**COST**

➛ $5 per vehicle. There are fees for the rentals; call the park or visit its website for details.

**GETTING THERE**

➛ By car, take U.S. Hwy. 93 S. Drive south for about 24 miles until you see signs for Lake Mead National Recreation Area. Free parking on site. About 45 minutes from McCarran International Airport.

➛ By public transit, no regular service exists. Grayline Las Vegas (800-634-6579), Quality Tours of Las Vegas (702-631-2292) and other tour bus companies make the run from Las Vegas.

**NEARBY**

➛ Hoover Dam, Arizona border, town of Boulder City.

**COMMENT**

➛ Even if you don't plan to do any swimming, Lake Mead is worth seeing simply for its beauty. Plan a 2-hour visit.

# *See it Like a New Yorker*
# MANHATTAN EXPRESS

**New York-New York, 3790 Las Vegas Blvd. S., Las Vegas**
**(702) 740-6969**
**www.nynyhotelcasino.com**

Here's a whole new way to see New York or New York-New York. The Manhattan Express is the centerpiece of the resort's amusement area. Designed to resemble a Coney Island coaster, it's long, high, fast and has two loops. Departing from inside the resort, the coaster takes riders high above one of the busiest intersections in Las Vegas—Tropicana and Las Vegas boulevards. The MGM Grand and Tropicana are across the street in one direction, the spires of the Excalibur in another. Passengers zip by too quickly to appreciate much of the view.

The coaster passes above replicas of the Statue of Liberty, Hudson River and 12 New York City landmarks, including the Empire State, Chrysler and Seagrams buildings. It also travels through part of the resort's interior, which uncannily resembles many areas of New York. The ride thrills kids and that's its real attraction. Negative gravity and a 180-degree heartline twist-and-dive-rolling maneuver will do that.

The Manhattan Express is designed for thrill-seekers 54 inches and taller, but there's plenty for younger kids to do in the Coney Island Emporium.

Techno-attractions, including laser tag, simulators and virtual-reality games, and old-fashioned delights such as skee ball, bumper cars and a shooting gallery await. The Coney Island Emporium is a family attraction; kids younger than 18 can't be in the arcade without a parent or guardian after 10 pm on school nights, or midnight on weekends and summer nights.

**SEASONS AND TIMES**

➛ Year-round (weather permitting): Sun–Thu, 10 am–11 pm; Fri–Sat, 10 am–11:30 pm.

**COST**

➛ $10 per person.

**GETTING THERE**

➛ By car, take I-15 N. to the Tropicana Blvd. E. Exit. Travel east on Tropicana. The hotel entrance is just before the intersection of Las Vegas Blvd. Free parking on site. About 10 minutes from McCarran International Airport.

➛ By public transit, take city bus route 301. It stops along Las Vegas Blvd.

**NEARBY**

➛ MGM Grand, Tropicana, Excalibur.

**COMMENT**

➛ Walk the kids through the resort's interior to get a taste of New York. Plan a 1-hour visit.

## *An Excellent Adventure*
# MGM GRAND ADVENTURES

**3799 Las Vegas Blvd. S., Las Vegas**
**(702) 891-7979**
**www.mgmgrand.com**

MGM Grand Adventures is the park that gave people the idea that Las Vegas was re-creating itself as a family destination.

Like any good theme park, this one is divided into rides for kids, teens and adult thrill-seekers. The ultimate thrill ride is the Sky Screamer. Passengers are harnessed, lifted 220 feet into the sky and released into free fall, hence the name "screamer." The park offers plenty of amusements with family appeal, including a roller coaster. Despite the name, Lightning Bolt is a relatively gentle ride that moves through much of the lush landscaping of the park. Grand Canyon Rapids, the center of much of that greenery, is a free-floating raft ride. Over the Edge is a flume ride that promises everyone a rumbling, splashing good time. Paddle boats, bumper cars, kiddie rides, remote-control boats and games such as basketball shoot and a shooting gallery round out the selection.

The park has shows and other performances throughout the day, including the Dueling Pirates Stunt Spectacular. Don't miss the live entertainment that's put on in the Gold Rush Theatre, Magic Screen Theatre, Star Steppin' Stage and Show Place Junction.

**SEASONS AND TIMES**

→ Spring—Fall: Daily. Seasonal hours; call or visit the website for specific dates and times.

**COST**

→ Individuals: $12.95. Sky Screamer (priced separately, includes park admission): Triple flyers $35, double flyers $30, single flyers $25. Seasonal pass: $42.95.

**GETTING THERE**

→ By car, take I-15 N. to Tropicana Blvd. E. Travel east on Tropicana and cross Las Vegas Blvd. Free parking on site. About 10 minutes from McCarran International Airport.

→ By public transit, take city bus route 301. It stops along Las Vegas Blvd.

**NEARBY**

→ New York-New York, Tropicana, Excalibur.

**COMMENT**

→ The park is small. A misting system provides relief on hot days, and there's heat for when it's cooler. Plan a 3-hour visit.

## *A Proper Thrill*
# PRIMADONNA RESORTS

**I-15 S., Primm**
**(702) 382-1212**
**www.primadonna.com**

At 5,483 feet long and with a run time of 2 minutes, 43 seconds—the Desperado at Buffalo Bill's is one thrilling ride. But it's not all that Primadonna Resorts has to offer. The Adventure Canyon log flume has the added attraction of laser-equipped pistols so passengers can shoot threatening targets they pass along the way. This is one ride the entire family can enjoy.

The Ghost Town Motion Simulator Theaters bring you a variety of spooky adventures. The Turbo Drop makes you feel as though the bottom has dropped out of the world at 45 miles per hour. For thrill-ride junkies who want to keep their feet on the ground, there's the MaxFlight VR2002 virtual roller coaster.

The real star of the show is the Desperado—it is among the world's tallest and fastest roller coasters with a drop of 225 feet. After Desperado leaves the station, it climbs impossibly high before plunging into a mine-tunnel entrance, taking a hard right and then zipping and zooming over curves and hills. At three points, riders feel near-zero gravity.

The resort has video game rooms and nearby there is a Fashion Outlet where families can do some serious shopping.

**SEASONS AND TIMES**

➛ Year-round (weather permitting): Sun—Thu, 10 am—10 pm; Fri—Sat, 10 am—midnight.

**COST**

➛ Admission: Free. Rides (per person): Adventure Canyon Log Flume, MaxFlight VR2002 Virtual Roller Coaster and motion-simulator theaters $4, Turbo Drop $5, Desperado Roller Coaster $6.

**GETTING THERE**

➛ By car, take I-15 S. to Primm. The resorts are on both sides of the road and connected by a shuttle. Free parking on site. About 45 minutes from McCarran International Airport.

➛ By public transit, shuttles run from some Las Vegas locations to the Fashion Outlet of Las Vegas, which is near Primadonna Resorts (call 888-424-0898 for schedule information).

**NEARBY**

→ Fashion Outlet of Las Vegas, California border.

**COMMENT**

→ Primm—which consists of resorts—is an interesting enclave to explore, with shops, restaurants and scheduled entertainment. Plan 2 hours for visiting for the park; longer if you want to look around Primm.

# Now you can Experience **SPEED: THE RIDE**

**Sahara, 2535 Las Vegas Blvd. S., Las Vegas**
**(702) 737-2111**

The newest of the coasters to be built along the Las Vegas Strip features the shortest track, but don't let that fool you—Speed: The Ride packs a mean punch. The secret is in the magnetrons that drive the ride; most coasters use the force of gravity for power. Those standing in line get an idea of Speed's power as it shoots out of the station on departure.

Speed dips underground through fog, does a loop, passes through the Sahara's sign and then shoots up a vertical tower, giving passengers a view of nothing but the sky. Then just as their hearts begin to beat again, Speed covers the same track—in reverse. Thanks to the magnetrons, it moves just as fast.

Riders have to be at least 54 inches tall to go on

Speed. But thrill-loving kids ages eight and older will be crazy about this ride. Afterward, families can check out gear at Sahara's NASCAR café, or take in Steve Wyrick's magic show.

**SEASONS AND TIMES**

→ Year-round (weather permitting): Sun—Thu, 11 am—10 pm; Fri—Sat, 11 am—midnight.

**COST**

→ Individuals: $8 ($6 for Nevada residents).

**GETTING THERE**

→ By car, take I-15 N. to the Sahara Ave. E. Exit. Travel east on Sahara to where it intersects Las Vegas Blvd. The hotel is at the intersection. Free parking on site. About 20 minutes from McCarran International Airport.

→ By public transit, take city bus route 301. It stops along Las Vegas Blvd.

**NEARBY**

→ Wet 'n Wild, Stratosphere, Las Vegas Hilton, Circus Circus.

**COMMENT**

→ This ride lives up to its name. Plan a 30-minute visit.

# *Seeing the Stars*
# THE LAS VEGAS 51s

**Cashman Field, 850 Las Vegas Blvd. N., Las Vegas**
**(702) 798-7825**
**www.lasvegasstars.com**

A number of people are under the mistaken impression that there is no old-fashioned fun in Las Vegas. Well, how does baseball grab you? Baseball played by the Las Vegas 51s, the AAA affiliate of the Los Angeles Dodgers.

The 51s play at Cashman Field, a 9,334-seat, government-owned facility near downtown. Seating at the field comes in every variety from bleachers (with backs) to regular stadium-style seats that place you closer to the play. Small enough to provide an up-close-and-personal setting, the stadium is the perfect spot to bring the family and watch a minor-league ball game.

As in the case with all minor-league teams, the 51s know how to plan the promotions that will bring out the fans. Throwing T-shirts and candy into the crowd, passing out free Cracker Jacks™ and mini-bats and staging between-the-innings field-level competitions for bigger prizes are always fan favorites.

**SEASONS AND TIMES**

➛ June—Sept: Games usually start at 7:05 pm. Call or visit the website for specific dates and times.

**COST**

➛ Individual tickets: $5 to $8. Available at the ticket counter and other locations around town.

**GETTING THERE**

➛ By car, take I-15 N. to U.S. Hwy. 95 E. Travel east on Hwy. 95 and take the Las Vegas Blvd. Exit. Turn north and travel 2 blocks to the stadium. Parking on site. About 30 minutes from McCarran International Airport.

➛ By public transit, take city bus route 401 to the stadium.

**NEARBY**

➛ Cashman Center, Lied Discovery Children's Museum, Las Vegas Natural History Museum.

**COMMENT**

➛ The 51s' season extends from late spring until early fall when the weather gets hot. Gentle breezes waft through the hilltop stadium to keep it comfortable. The misting system also provides relief.

## *Wild About* WET 'N WILD

**2601 Las Vegas Blvd. S., Las Vegas**
**(702) 734-0088**
**www.wetnwild.com/las-vegas**

Wet 'n Wild Waterparks are located in various parts of the country, but the one on the Las Vegas Strip features a ride with a distinct Vegas touch. Called the Royal Flush, it's billed as "the ultimate swirly." In this attraction, bathers feel as though they've entered a giant toilet bowl, spinning around the rim at speeds of 45 miles per hour. They have a choice of two rides: fully enclosed, or open to the air.

Then there's the Black Hole, a two-person raft ride; the Bomb Bay, where riders are launched from a bomber-like vertical tunnel 76 feet up; the intertwining slides of the Blue Niagra; Der Stuka, which the park promises is the fastest water slide in the world; and much more.

There are plenty of rides for guppies too. Miniature versions of the park's more daunting attractions, plus water-oriented playground equipment and kid-size tables and chairs are in the aptly named Kids' Park. Families can ride the park's easy-going attractions, including a wave pool, a lazy river and Willy Willy, a circular whirlpool-like ride named for an Australian whirlwind.

Though they can never replace the attention of a vigilant parent, the park is staffed with certified lifeguards.

**SEASONS AND TIMES**

➛ Apr—early Oct: Daily. Hours vary by the month; call or visit the website for specific dates and times.

**COST**

➛ Individuals: $25.95, children (less than 48 inches tall) $19.95, under 3 free. Season's passes: $95. Half-price admission and season passes for senior citizens. Discount coupons available at numerous outlets, such as fast-food outlets and supermarkets in the Las Vegas area.

**GETTING THERE**

➛ By car, take I-15 N. to the Sahara Ave. E. Exit. Travel east on Sahara to Las Vegas Blvd. and turn south. Wet 'n Wild will be just south of the Sahara. Free parking on site. About 20 minutes from McCarran International Airport.

→ By public transit, take city bus route 301. It stops along Las Vegas Blvd.

**NEARBY**
→ Sahara, Stratosphere, Las Vegas Hilton.

**COMMENT**
→ A great place for an outdoor family day. Get there early and stake your claim on the lounge chairs, especially if you want a spot in the shade.

# *Other Places to Play*

## PAINTBALL

**DESERT STORM PAINTBALL GAMES**
**1 mile after the end of the asphalt off North Jones Blvd., Las Vegas**
**(702) 595-2555**

**VEGAS INDOOR PAINTBALL ARENA (VIPA)**
**2750 S. Highland Dr., Las Vegas**
**(702) 893-8472**

## GO-CARTING

**DANSEY'S INDOOR RACE TRACK**
**741 N. Nellis Blvd., Las Vegas**
**(702) 453-7223**

**LAS VEGAS MINI GRAND PRIX**
**1401 N. Rainbow Blvd., Las Vegas**
**(702) 259-7000**

## LASER TAG

**LASERFORCE**
**Suite 100, 6330 S. Pecos Rd., Las Vegas**
**(702) 320-1774**

**LASER QUEST**
**7361 W. Lake Mead Blvd., Las Vegas**
**(702) 243-8881**

## ICE-SKATING

### CRYSTAL PALACE SKATING CENTER
4680 Boulder Hwy., Las Vegas (702) 458-7107
9295 W. Flamingo Rd., Las Vegas (702) 253-9832
3901 N. Rancho Dr., Las Vegas (702) 645-4892

### LAS VEGAS ICE ARENA
7675 Sultana St., Las Vegas
(702) 260-7465

### LAS VEGAS ICE GARDENS
3896 Swenson St., Las Vegas
(702) 731-1062

### SAHARA ICE PALACE
800 Karen Ave., Las Vegas
(702) 260-7465

### SANTA FE ICE ARENA
4949 N. Rancho Dr., Las Vegas
(702) 658-4993

## FAMILY ACTIVITY CENTERS

### MOUNTASIA
2050 Olympic Ave., Henderson
(702) 454-4386

### SCANDIA FAMILY FUN CENTER
2900 Sirius Ave., Las Vegas
(702) 364-0070

### ATHLETIC ARTS ACADEMY
6150 Annie Oakley, Las Vegas
(702) 450-2787

## MINIATURE GOLF

### THE GREENS OF LAS VEGAS
Tropicana at Paradise, Las Vegas
(702) 949-2000

Chapter 5

# PLACES TO LEARN

# *Introduction*

Part of the fun of parenting is satisfying your children's endless curiosity about the world around them. There are many sites in the Las Vegas area that will help you do this in a entertaining way. This chapter includes activities where kids can see chocolate and candies being made, learn about astronomy, visit a hydro-electric dam, watch race cars being assembled, tour a vineyard and find out how to grow a garden in the desert. All of it adds up to lots of learning and fun for the whole family. Another plus for Mom and Dad is that most of these attractions are free, or at least easy on the pocketbook—just don't tell the kids they're educational.

## *How Does Your Garden Grow?*

# DESERT DEMONSTRATION GARDENS

**3701 W. Alta Dr., Las Vegas**
**(702) 258-3205**
**www.lvvwd.com/conservation/ddg/ddg.html**

Here's a double lesson for kids—especially those new to Las Vegas. Desert landscapes are far from bleak. In fact, kids can learn to make them lush and green while conserving water. These lessons are brought home at the Desert Demonstration Gardens, a public service of the Southern Nevada Water Authority. The Gardens feature more than 1,000 species of water-loathing plants in 11 theme settings. Staff are on hand to tell you about the flora Thursdays to Saturdays, from 9 am to 1 pm. Of particular interest to the younger set will be the kids' garden, established by 8- to 12-year-old 4-H'ers who are interested in desert gardening. They plant vegetables, experiment with native varieties and use drip irrigation, organic fertilizer and natural pest-control methods. This is also the home of the Five-Star Worm Hotel. Beware of the cactus garden; its signs warn you that the plants "bite."

Children are often taken with the spectacular plant life arrayed around a desert arroyo, a rose garden, a courtyard and other gardens. Best of all, they are encouraged to roam freely along the paths that crisscross and encircle the plants. They just might be inspired to start their own garden when they get home. Make sure you stop by the visitor center. It's a source of information on all types of gardening in the desert. You can learn about efficient watering techniques, too. Periodic free workshops, tours, classes and programs, such as the annual Meet the Experts, add to the enjoyment level for the whole family.

**SEASONS AND TIMES**

→ Year-round: Daily, 8 am—5 pm. Closed most holidays.

**COST**

→ Free.

**GETTING THERE**

→ By car, take I-95 N. to U.S. 95 and continue north to the Valley View Dr. Exit. Head south on Valley View to Alta Dr. and turn east. The gardens are on the corner of Alta and Valley View. Free parking on site. About 30 minutes from McCarran International Airport.

→ By public transit, take city bus route route 207.

**NEARBY**

→ Southern Nevada Zoological Park, Nevada State Museum and Historical Society.

**COMMENT**

→ This is a great place for kids to burn off steam. Plan a 1-hour visit.

# *Decidedly Delicious*
# ETHEL M CHOCOLATES™

**2 Cactus Garden (at Sunset Way and Mountain Vista), Henderson**
**(702) 433-2500**
**www.ethelm.com**

If there's a serious chocolate lover in the family—and what kid isn't—this place is for you. Ethel M came into being in 1981, when veteran candy maker Forrest Mars created a premium chocolate line in Las Vegas and named it to honor his mother.

Ethel M chocolates are available worldwide through the company's catalog, its Internet site and in shops throughout Las Vegas. But the best way to discover these delectables is to drop by the factory just a few miles from the Strip. Kids can follow the candy-production line to see how chocolates are made. If the timing is right, they get an up-close-and-personal demonstration complete with a free sample. Another free sample awaits you in the gift shop. This time, visitors get to choose their treat from dozens of varieties. Looking for something for that someone special? The gift shop offers custom-designed boxes and seasonal items, many of them geared to kids.

Top off your visit with a quick stroll through Ethel M's cactus garden. It has more than 300 varieties. The cacti themselves are off-limits, but the wide path that winds through them is a great place for kids to learn more about these fascinating plants as they burn off that sugar.

**SEASONS AND TIMES**

→ Year-round: Daily, 8:30 am—7 pm.

**COST**

→ Free.

**GETTING THERE**

→ By car, take I-215 E. to the Sunset Rd. Exit. Go east on Sunset to the point where it turns sharply south. Continue straight onto Sunset Way. The factory is on the north side of the road. Free parking on site. About 15 minutes from McCarran International Airport.

→ By public transit, take city bus route route 212.

**NEARBY**

→ Ron Lee's World of Clowns, All-American SportPark, Hoover Dam.

**COMMENT**

→ Consider combining this with Ron Lee's World of Clowns or the National Vitamin Co. Plan a 1-hour visit.

## *Seeing Water Become Power at* HOOVER DAM

**U.S. 93, Boulder City**
**(702) 294-3524**
**www.hooverdam.com**

Simply getting a gander at the Hoover Dam and learning how it is used to generate electricity from water, would prove educational for most kids. But add a behind-the-scenes tour and see the additional enjoyment and knowledge kids gain. Visitors pack into huge elevators to ascend to an observation deck overlooking the generator floor, where eight massive hydroelectric generators are constantly working. Above the dull roar, a guide explains that together with the nine generators on the Arizona side of the dam, Hoover produces enough electricity to service 1.3 million people. Then it's down the stairs, through a door and outside for a view looking up the 726-foot-high dam, the fourth largest in the world.

Later, the guide will lead you inside a tunnel (used to divert the Colorado River while the dam was being built in the 1930s) and explain how the intake towers in Lake Mead above the dam supply the water that runs the generators. You will also learn that the whole structure is designed to make electricity and to control the mighty river, which before being dammed regularly produced flood and drought conditions in the area. After the tour, you can study exhibits on dam construction and operations in the visitor center and go onto the observation deck. It offers sweeping views of Hoover Dam and the surrounding canyons.

**SEASONS AND TIMES**

→ Visitors center: Year-round, daily, 8 am—5:45 pm. Tours: Year-round, daily, 8:30 am—5:15 pm. Closed Thanksgiving and Christmas.

**COST**

→ Exhibit-only tickets: Individuals $4, under 7 free. Traditional tours: Individuals (17 to 61) $8, seniors (62 and older) $7, youths (7 to 16) $2, under 7 free. Extended hard-hat tours: $25 per person.

**GETTING THERE**

➛ By car, take I-215 E. to U.S. 93 and follow U.S. 93 south through Boulder City until you see signs for parking near the dam. Pay parking on site ($3). About 45 minute from McCarran International Airport.

**NEARBY**

➛ Boulder City historic district, Boulder City-Hoover Dam Museum.

**COMMENT**

➛ To help younger kids enjoy the visit, explain the basics to them beforehand. Plan a 2- to 3-hour visit.

## *Visiting Candy Land*
## M&M'S™ WORLD

**Showcase Mall, 3785 Las Vegas Blvd. S., Las Vegas**
**(702) 736-7611**
**www.m-ms.com/store/3d**

Ever wonder how the chocolate gets inside the "melts in your mouth, not in your hands" candy shell of an M&M™? Here's your chance to find out. For the ultimate experience, attend M&M's™ Academy beforehand. There, visitors learn about coloring, buffing and drying, plus fun fictional stuff about the requirements these colorful little candy stars must meet. The Academy visit concludes with an animated 3-D film that recounts the misadventures of Red and Peanut Yellow—a couple of M&Ms™ trying to reclaim the "M" that Red lost at the gaming tables. A human actress plays Candace "Candy" Mann, your host. It's fun and there's a bit of a lesson for kids.

Appropriately enough, M&M's™ World sells all things M&M™, including clothing and accessories, desk sets, toys and sporting equipment. Kids will be dazzled as they wander through three floors of merchandise, much of it arranged by color. The World also has tall clear dispensers of M&Ms™ (plain and peanut) with all the standard colors, plus a few you can't get anywhere else—white, teal and violet. The per-pound prices are higher than at the supermarket, but the novelty of creating their own color combination will appeal to most kids.

**SEASONS AND TIMES**

→ M&M's™ World: Year-round, Sun—Thu, 10 am—midnight; Fri—Sat, 10 am—1 am. M&M's™ Academy: Year-round, Sun—Thu, 11 am—6:20 pm; Fri—Sat, 10:30 am—8 pm.

**COST**

→ M&M's™ World: Free to browse. M&M's™ Academy: $3 per person.

**GETTING THERE**

→ By car, take I-15 N. to the Tropicana Ave. E. Exit. Head east on Tropicana to Las Vegas Blvd. S. Park at the MGM Grand. Walk through the MGM Grand and then north about 1/2 block on Las Vegas. About 15 minutes from McCarran International Airport.

→ By public transit, take city bus route 301.

**NEARBY**

→ New York-New York, the Luxor, MGM Grand.

**COMMENT**

→ Consider combining this with the Lion Habitat at MGM Grand or the Manhattan Express roller coaster and arcade at New York-New York. Plan a 1-hour visit.

# *Open Wide*
# THE NATIONAL VITAMIN CO.

**Suite 210, 7440 S. Industrial Rd., Las Vegas**
**(702) 269-9600**
**www.nationalvitamin.com**

Here's one question that always fascinates kids and stumps most adults: how do they get the powder into the little vitamin capsules without spilling it? You will learn the answer during the National Vitamin Co. tour. Families follow the production line and look through big plate-glass windows at the various stages of tablet, capsule and softgel production. It's highly automated, though visitors can see workers performing quality tests on the products.

In the tablet-production area, everyone is fascinated watching the powder being compressed into a mold to become the right shape. It is then bounced and jiggled along a series of screens until smooth and the right size. Ever wonder how softgels are manufactured? You'll find out by watching softgel grains melt. The goo is then spun into ribbons and punched into ovals. Two ovals are injected with a vitamin and joined into one unit, which continues along the line being polished as it goes. Across from the production windows, there is a series of displays on the importance of nutrients in proper human development. At the end of the tour, visitors receive free samples of skin-care cream and a multivitamin from the company's Dino-Life™ line of chewable multivitamins for kids.

**SEASONS AND TIMES**

➛ Year-round: Mon—Sat, 8:30 am—6 pm; Sun, 11 am—5 pm.

**COST**

➛ Free.

**GETTING THERE**

➛ By car, take I-15 S. to Blue Diamond Rd. Go west on Blue Diamond to Industrial Rd. Turn north and drive for about 1/2 mile to the factory, which is on the east side of the road. Free parking on site. About 15 minutes from McCarran International Airport.

**NEARBY**

➛ Ethel M Chocolates™, McCarran International Airport, All-American Sport Park.

**COMMENT**

➛ Consider combining this with Ethel M Chocolates™ and Ron Lee's World of Clowns. Plan a 30-minute visit.

## *Toast of the Town*

# PAHRUMP VALLEY VINEYARDS

**3810 Winery Rd., Pahrump**
**(775) 727-6900**

A winery in the Mohave Desert? No doubt about it, the novelty alone makes the Pahrump Valley Vineyards worth the visit, but there's plenty to see and do. Visitors tour the facility and learn about wine-making—from watching the juice being loaded into tanks for aging to seeing the machines that insert corks into bottles. Guides are knowledgeable and seem particularly patient in answering kids' questions. Smaller kids will giggle when they hear about the time wild horses from the surrounding mountains visited the vineyards. Deciding that the grapes tasted pretty good, they spread the message to their jackrabbit friends and together they devoured the entire crop. Pahrump's re-planted after erecting a tall fence. However, until the new plants are ready, they will make their wine using grape juice from California.

The tour includes visiting the third-floor tower of the winery, which offers a commanding view of the valley and the surrounding Spring Mountains. Kids will have to skip the free tasting, but they can have a soft drink as they follow along. Families interested in buying wine for gifts can have a personal message printed on the label. The winery has a bright, airy restaurant and the lovely grounds feature an old-fashioned gazebo, among other things.

**SEASONS AND TIMES**

➛ Winery tours: Year-round, daily, 10 am–4 pm. The restaurant serves lunch (noon to 3 pm) and dinner (5 pm to 9 pm) daily.

**COST**

➛ Winery tours: Free.

**GETTING THERE**

➛ By car, take I-15 S. to the Blue Diamond Rd. Exit. Access State Rd. 160 and take it west to the outskirts of Pahrump. Turn east on Winery Rd. Free parking on site. About an hour from McCarran International Airport.

**NEARBY**

➛ Red Rock Canyon, Death Valley National Monument.

**COMMENT**

➛ Plan a 2- to 3-hour visit for the tour, tasting and stroll of the grounds; more if you want to dine (reservations advised).

# *Star-gazing at* THE PLANETARIUM

**Community College of Southern Nevada**
**3200 E. Cheyenne Ave., Las Vegas**
**(702) 651-4759**
**www.ccsn.nevada.edu/planetarium**

Two celestial shows are always in rotation at the Planetarium. A popular one for local youngsters is Sky Watch, which brings home the night sky to observers. Their anticipation builds as the domed ceiling of the planetarium is darkened and then covered with the constellations kids can see from their own backyards. Later in the show, they observe the difference in star watching out in the desert where the city's lights are but a distant glow.

The hour-long program is accompanied by recorded, running commentary and includes a hit parade of famous highlights of the night sky, such as the Milky Way (rarely visible from Las Vegas because of the ambient light), Orion's Belt and various planets. Especially interesting is the segment that demonstrates how some of the planets would look to the naked eye with a low-powered backyard telescope compared to an observatory model. The show might be boring for the youngest kids and those who have no interest in the night sky. But then again, even tots may be bedazzled at this closer look at nature's gems.

#### SEASONS AND TIMES

→ Showings: Year-round, Fri, 6 pm and 7:30 pm; Sat, 3:30 pm and 7:30 pm.

#### COST

→ Adults $4, seniors, community college students and children $3.

#### GETTING THERE

→ By car, take I-15 N. to the Cheyenne Ave. Exit and head west. The planetarium is on the Cheyenne campus of the Community College of Southern Nevada, on the north side of the road. There are signs. Free parking on site. About 40 minutes from McCarran International Airport.

→ By public transit, take city bus route 218.

#### NEARBY

→ The Las Vegas Motor Speedway, Shelby American Sports Car Museum and Assembly Area.

#### COMMENT

→ For more fun, schedule an evening show and venture out afterward for some supervised time with the college's telescopes. Plan a 2-hour visit.

# *Send in the Clowns*
# RON LEE'S WORLD OF CLOWNS

**330 Carousel Pkwy., Henderson**
**(702) 434-1700**
**www.ronlee.com**

This stop is first and foremost a factory tour. But kids won't be able to resist what's produced here—clowns embellished with gold and resting on stone slabs for collectors around the world.

Ron Lee's also produces Disney-licensed items, some very detailed and ornate, such as the Venetian canal scene from *The Lady and the Tramp*. Older kids are fascinated to walk along the production line and learn how the figures are made. They can watch a worker take a mold, add some liquid pewter and then, using centrifugal force, cast a statue. Next they'll see the cast pieces being cut from the molds and then soldered and polished. Other employees paint the figures, apply gold leaf and make them ready for shipping. All along the production line, TV monitors help make things more understandable by explaining each step in the process.

There's plenty here for the youngest visitors too. The World of Clowns takes its theme seriously. Kids can ride the carousel and visit two elaborate animated dioramas; drop a quarter in one and a circus scene comes to life. They'll also see clown memorabilia, including trunks, costumes, shoes and dozens of clown portraits.

**SEASONS AND TIMES**

→ Year-round: Mon—Fri, 8:30 am—4:30 pm; Sat, 10 am—4:30 pm.

**COST**

→ Admission: Free. Carousel tickets $1.

**GETTING THERE**

→ By car, take I-215 E. to the Sunset Rd. Exit. Head east on Sunset to Stephanie St. and turn south. Continue on Stephanie to Warm Springs Rd. and turn east. Carousel Pkwy. will be the 4th street on the south side of the road. Free parking on site. About 30 minutes from McCarran International Airport.

→ By public transit, take city bus route 217.

**NEARBY**

→ Ethel M Chocolates™, Hoover Dam.

**COMMENT**

→ Consider combining this with Ethel M Chocolates™ or National Vitamin Co. Plan a 1-hour visit.

# *zooming off to the* SHELBY AMERICAN SPORTS CAR MUSEUM AND ASSEMBLY AREA

**6755 Speedway Blvd., Las Vegas**
**(702) 643-3000**
**www.carrollshelby.com**

Gentlemen (and ladies) start your engines and head for the Las Vegas Motor Speedway. Car lovers and future racers will get to see more than a dozen Shelby American vehicles arrayed in a shiny rainbow of bright colors.

Carroll Shelby was a veteran racecar driver who was in failing health when he retired from racing in the 1960s. From there, he went on to create his first racecar. The rest, as they say, is history. His Shelby American Cobras and Shelby Mustangs went on to become highly successful racing cars. In the early 90s, Shelby moved his operations to Las Vegas. Examples of Shelby's most noteworthy models are on display in the museum. Most of them reflect his early practice of modifying other automakers' vehicles to create the cars he wanted. The museum has a couple of Shelby American's current original-production classics—the Cobra and the Series 1, valued at $175,000.

This is more than a museum. It is also a working auto-assembly plant. Visitors can see the cars in every stage of production and learn how they are put together. The on-site gift shop has all things automotive, including hats and T-shirts with Shelby's name or likeness on it. For an extra thrill, take in the morning tour and attend a race at the nearby Las Vegas Motor Speedway afterward.

**SEASONS AND TIMES**

➛ Year-round: Mon—Fri, 8 am—5 pm. Tours: 10:30 am or by appointment at 3:30 pm.

**COST**

➛ Free.

**GETTING THERE**

➛ By car, take I-15 N. to the Las Vegas Motor Speedway Exit. The Shelby building is on the south side of Speedway Blvd., about 1/4 mile down the road. Free parking on site. About 45 minutes from McCarran International Airport.

➛ By public transit, the Speedway Shuttle goes to the Las Vegas Motor Speedway from the city bus Downtown Transportation Center during special events only.

**NEARBY**

➛ The Las Vegas Motor Speedway, the Planetarium at the Cheyenne Campus of the Community College of Southern Nevada.

**COMMENT**

➛ Plan a 1-hour visit.

CHAPTER 6

# MUSIC, THEATER, DANCE AND CINEMA

# Introduction

Las Vegas is famous—or maybe that should be infamous—for its adults-only shows. But there are a surprising number of performances that are both family-friendly and entertaining.

Some are classics, such as the World's Greatest Circus Acts, Siegfried & Roy, the Tournament of Kings and Madame Tussaud's Celebrity Encounter. Some are cultural, such as the Nevada Ballet Theatre, while others are artsy, Cirque du Soleil's *O* or the Blue Man Group, for example. And then there's the Masquerade Show in the Sky with its only-in-Vegas style.

Many of them are expensive for families, so save your pennies and keep your eyes peeled for deals, such as two-for-one Nevada-resident specials. There's one thing all these shows have in common—each is worthy of a family night out.

# *In Living Color*
# BLUE MAN GROUP: LIVE AT LUXOR

**Luxor, 3900 Las Vegas Blvd. S., Las Vegas**
**(702) 262-4000**
**www.luxor.com**

Anyone who's seen the Blue Man Group perform at the Luxor says the same thing: the show is impossible to describe.

What can you say about a show where three grown men—coated in bright blue to the very edges of their eyelids—sit on stage munching cereal in rhythm? Or a show where paintings are created by splashing paint? Where else would you see three guys playing (as in musical instrument) huge tangles of plastic pipe?

The key to enjoying a performance by this high-energy trio is to not try to understand their antics—just sit back and enjoy. The Luxor bills this as a family show, although because of some somewhat startling effects, it's restricted to those five and older. And indeed, most kids will get a charge out of the on-stage performance.

The tone is set before the curtain rises when a staffer stops by each section, delivering pieces of what looks like toilet paper that audience members must wear somewhere on their bodies. They're also instructed to cheer by section.

This is a multi-media show with lots of booming drums (the Blue Men's music earned them a Grammy™ nomination), reader boards with messages that prompt the audience to dissolve into laughter, high-tech lighting and special live camera effects. There are pipes that dangle from the ceiling. And toilet paper that flows from the back of the audience to the front . . . you have to see it to understand it.

**SEASONS AND TIMES**

➛ Sat–Mon and Wed, 7 pm and 10 pm; Tue and Thu, 7 pm; Fri, 10 pm.

**COST**

➛ $55 and $65 per person.

**GETTING THERE**

➛ By car, take I-15 N. to Tropicana Blvd. E. Head east on Tropicana to Las Vegas Blvd. S. and turn south. The Luxor is the big glass pyramid on the west side of the road. Free parking on site. About 15 minutes from McCarran International Airport.

➛ By public transit, take city bus route 301.

**NEARBY**

➛ Excalibur, New York-New York, MGM Grand.

**COMMENT**

➛ The show lasts about 2 hours with intermissions.

*Rubbing Shoulders with VIPs*

# MADAME TUSSAUD'S CELEBRITY ENCOUNTER

**Venetian, 3355 Las Vegas Blvd. S., Las Vegas**
**(702) 414-1000**
**www.venetian.com**

Here's your chance to take the kids to one of those glitzy celebrity-laden parties. Madame Tussaud's Celebrity Encounter at the Venetian features wax figures of more than 100 past and present celebrities, in the fine Madame Tussaud's tradition. In Las Vegas however, Madame Tussaud's isn't the don't-touch proposition it is in other parts of the world. Visitors are invited to sidle up to Cher, get their pictures taken with their arm around Babe Ruth, or stick their finger in Jerry Springer's face.

The figures are arranged in room settings. Visitors are invited to the party of The Big Night, one of those high-profile Hollywood things where they'll see Brad Pitt and Oprah Winfrey among others. There's a sports section, a music area, a Las Vegas-theme section, an area recounting the history of Madame Tussaud's and a grand finale.

Madame Tussaud's Celebrity Encounter is cavalier about visitors touching their exact-double figures. Each night after the attraction closes, a fleet of workers moves in to repair any damage, accidental or otherwise.

**SEASONS AND TIMES**

➛ Year-round: Daily, 10 am—10 pm.

**COST**

➛ General admission $13.50, Nevada residents and seniors $11.50, children (4 to 12) $10.75, under 4 free.

**GETTING THERE**

➛ By car, take I-15 N. to the Spring Mountain Rd. E. Exit. Head east on Spring Mountain to Las Vegas Blvd. S. and turn south. The Venetian is visible on the east side of the road. Free parking on site. About 20 minutes from McCarran International Airport.

➛ By public transit, take city bus route 301.

**NEARBY**

➛ The Mirage, Harrah's, the Flamingo, Caesars Palace.

**COMMENT**

➛ Plan at least a 1-hour visit. Consider combining this with a ride on one of the Venetian's gondolas.

*The Pinnacle of Entertainment*

# MASQUERADE SHOW IN THE SKY

**Rio All-Suite Hotel & Casino, 3700 W. Flamingo Rd., Las Vegas (702) 252-7776**
**www.playrio.com**

Ever wanted to attend Mardi Gras but nervous about the raucous atmosphere? The Masquerade Show in the Sky at the Rio may be the next best thing.

It really is a show in the sky—or at least suspended from the soaring ceiling high above the Rio's casino. It's entertainment the whole family will enjoy. Four times a night, the samba music starts and five massive floats make their way around the area. People on the floats throw Mardi Gras-style beads to the crowds on the casino floor and the balconies above. See if your kids don't get into the swing of things! There's a different theme parade each hour. In addition to Mardi Gras, the shows celebrate Carnivale in Venice, Carnivale in Rio, a Venice Street Party and a Disco Swing Party.

The action's not just above. Various performers strut their stuff on the floor of the casino, including the dancer who keeps appearing and disappearing in the sunken center of a circular casino bar.

The parade area and casino are part of the Rio's Masquerade Village, a $200-million complex that includes shops and restaurants. Do your kids want to be part of the fun? For $9.95 each, visitors can ride along on the floats—costumed to fit the theme of the particular parade.

**SEASONS AND TIMES**

➛ Year-round: Daily, 4, 6, 8 and 10 pm.

**COST**

➛ Free to watch.

**GETTING THERE**

➛ By car, take I-15 N. to the Flamingo Rd. W. Exit. Head west on Flamingo; the resort is immediately visible on the north side of the road. Park in the Masquerade Village free parking garage for easiest access. About 20 minutes from McCarran International Airport.

➛ By public transit, take city bus route 202.

**NEARBY**

➛ Caesars Palace, Flamingo, Bellagio.

**COMMENT**

➛ Plan at least a 1-hour visit.

## *Best Foot Forward*
## NEVADA BALLET THEATRE

**Donald W. Reynolds Cultural Center,**
**1651 Inner Circle (Office), Las Vegas**
**(702) 243-2623**
**www.nevadaballet.com**

The Nevada Ballet Theatre, based in Summerlin (in northwestern Las Vegas), features a complex with rehearsal space for the professional troupe and an academy for aspiring dancers of all ages. Since 1983, the company has toured to more than 250 cities in 48 states. In Las Vegas, the troupe usually performs at the Judy Bayly Theater or Artemus Ham Hall on the campus of the University of Nevada, Las Vegas.

One of the company's most popular performances is that holiday staple, *The Nutcracker*. This compelling story with seasonal glitter and bits of magic is a great way to introduce children to dance.

But those who've seen *The Nutcracker* one too many times will find plenty more on the company's schedule, which runs from October through April.

Recent performances have included *Giselle, Fest Polanaise, Sleeping Beauty* and a Handel celebration. It's a great opportunity to expose those little boy band fans to the wonders and joys of the classics.

**SEASONS AND TIMES**

➛ Oct—Apr: Dates and times of the performances vary. Call the number above or visit the website for details.

**COST**

➛ Call for information.

**GETTING THERE**

➛ By car, to reach the UNLV campus (where most performances are held), take I-15 N. to the Tropicana Ave. E. Exit. Head east on Tropicana to Maryland Pkwy. and turn north. Follow Maryland to Cottage Grove Ave. and turn west. The halls are on the south side of the street. Free parking on site. About 20 minutes from McCarran International Airport.

➛ By public transit, take city bus route 109.

**NEARBY**

➛ Liberace Museum, the MGM Grand.

**COMMENT**

➛ Parking can be dicey. Arrive early, especially if attending a performance while UNLV classes are in session.

## *It's a Splash*

# O (CIRQUE DU SOLEIL)

**Bellagio, 3600 Las Vegas Blvd. S., Las Vegas**
**(702) 693-7111**
**www.bellagiolasvegas.com**

A hundred dollars per person for a show? Believe it or not, this one's worth it. *O* is easily among the best of Las Vegas' productions for families.

*O* comes from the creative geniuses at Cirque du Soleil. The theater at the Bellagio was built especially for it. The show is water-themed and that's apparent right away: it starts with some nifty and novel water effects on the part of a couple of Cirque du Soleil's ubiquitous clowns before the curtain even rises.

Once the main presentation begins, older audience members begin to understand why the show is expensive. It has got to be the latest engineering wonder of the world. Through what appears to be a set of hydraulically powered floor panels, the levels of the water on stage keep changing. During the course of the show, there's swimming, diving, appearances by boats, a house that floats by—even beached scuba divers. Don't try to figure it out. Just enjoy this outstanding production and revel in the variety of water-based special effects. The skill and artistry of the athletes, including divers, swimmers and dancers who perform on this unique stage is sublime, and the music at times haunting, other times peppy reminds you of water. A promise—the kids won't get bored.

**SEASONS AND TIMES**

→ Year-round: Fri–Tue, 7:30 pm and 10:30 pm.

**COST**

→ $93.50, $99 or $121 per person.

**GETTING THERE**

→ By car, take I-15 N. to the Flamingo Rd. E. Exit. Head east on Flamingo to Las Vegas Blvd. S. and turn south. The Bellagio is immediately on the west side of the road. Free parking on site. About 20 minutes from McCarran International Airport.

→ By public transit, take city bus route 301.

**NEARBY**

→ Caesars Palace, The Flamingo, Paris.

**COMMENT**

→ Plan a 3-hour visit. Kids are not normally allowed in the Bellagio, but will be if they have *O* tickets. Another Cirque du Soleil production called *Mystere* is presented at Treasure Island.

## *Time-honored Favorites*

# SIEGFRIED & ROY

**Mirage, 3400 Las Vegas Blvd. S., Las Vegas**
**(702) 791-7111**
**www.themirage.com**

To most people, this show is Las Vegas. Siegfried & Roy have been doing their schtick on the Strip since the late '60s. More than three million people have seen it so far.

What's the attraction? This was the first of the Strip magic shows, and while the genre is well represented in Las Vegas today by the likes of Lance Burton, Melinda (First Lady of Magic) and Steve Wyrick, nobody matches Siegfried & Roy's over-the-top style.

The costumes worn by Siegfried & Roy and the other 88 performers on stage may look a little dated. But in a way, that translates to pure classic camp for adults, while kids think they're pretty cool. The magic ("illusions," officially) is pretty impressive, though not awe-inspiring in these days of disappearing helicopters. Still, you've got to love a spectacle that includes lions and tigers appearing in glass boxes.

The animals are an integral part of Siegfried & Roy's production. Most impressive is a pyramid during the finale with the big cats on every tier. There isn't a lot of magic involved, but how they get those big cats to sit still is a wonder in itself. Add to that an elephant (at one point, Roy appears riding one) and lots of elaborate production acts starring dancers—this is classic family entertainment.

**SEASONS AND TIMES**

➛ Year-round: Sun—Mon, 7:30 pm; Tue, Fri—Sat, 7:30 and 11 pm.

**COST**

➛ $100.50 per person.

**GETTING THERE**

➛ By car, take I-15 N. to the Flamingo Rd. E. Exit. Head east on Flamingo to Las Vegas Blvd. S. and turn north. The Mirage is the second resort complex on the west side of the road. Free parking on site. About 20 minutes from McCarran International Airport.

➛ By public transit, take city bus route 301.

**NEARBY**

➛ Caesars Palace, the Flamingo, Harrah's.

**COMMENT**

➛ The show lasts about 2 hours.

## *Surely you Joust!*

# TOURNAMENT OF KINGS

**Excalibur Hotel-Casino, 3850 Las Vegas Blvd. S., Las Vegas**
**(702) 597-7700**
**www.excalibur-casino.com**

Dinner shows with horse acts may be old hat these days. But this one's so original (and so well produced) that it seems like a fresh idea.

In keeping with the Excalibur's medieval theme, the Tournament of Kings revolves around a number of kingdoms, each with its own king and all under the mantel of King Arthur. Diners, for example, get to sit in Ireland, Austria, France, Russia, Hungary and so on.

The plot involves a competition among the kings, all on horseback, to see who's the strongest and most skilled. In what may be a holdover from the Cold War, the Russian king is a bit of a bad boy and creates lots of crowd reaction. But the real villain is a fire-breathing evil dragon who leads his army in a battle against the combined kings.

Crowd interaction is a hallmark of the Tournament of Kings. Before the show, audience members are tutored in huzzahs, hisses and eating with your hands (in the tradition of such shows). But things aren't as messy as they could be with a menu of tomato soup (in a cup), roasted Cornish hen, broccoli spears and apple turnovers.

As the audience eats, the action in the ring continues. The kings eventually have to unite to help save King Arthur's domain. There's lots of riding, special effects and action of all sorts. Your kids will eat it up.

**SEASONS AND TIMES**

→ Year-round: Daily, 6 pm and 8:30 pm.

**COST**

→ $36.95 per person.

**GETTING THERE**

→ By car, take I-15 N. to the Tropicana Blvd. E. Exit. Head east on Tropicana to Las Vegas Blvd. S. and turn south. The resort is immediately on the west side of the road. Free parking on site. About 15 minutes from McCarran International Airport.

→ By public transit, take city bus route 301.

**NEARBY**

→ New York-New York, MGM Grand, Luxor, Mandalay Bay.

**COMMENT**

→ Plan at least a 2-hour visit.

# *Step Right Up to the* WORLD'S GREATEST CIRCUS ACTS

**Circus Circus, 2880 Las Vegas Blvd. S., Las Vegas**
**(702) 734-0410**
**www.circuscircus-lasvegas.com**

Here's your chance to see the circus—as much or as little as you want. The best thing is it's free.

Circus Circus, a landmark hotel-casino on the Strip, hosts circus acts in its second-floor arcade area. A different act is featured every half-hour, each performing for about 20 minutes. Usually five or six different performances take place on any given day. If you've got the time, kids can see practically a whole circus, including aerialists, clowns, high-wire walkers and others. Don't expect to see trained animals at Circus Circus. The featured acts usually showcase only human performers.

Attendance at the shows can vary greatly. Some limited bleacher seating is offered, but when the joint is jumping, expect to line up on the walkways around the ring with the rest of the crowd. This isn't the spacious environment of a three-ring circus; the area where the performers work is limited. However, that may be of benefit if you are planning a short visit. The bleachers offer the best view, however standing ringside puts kids near the center of the action.

**SEASONS AND TIMES**

➛ Year-round: Daily, every half-hour from 11 am—midnight.

**COST**

➛ Free.

**GETTING THERE**

➛ By car, take I-15 N. to the Sahara Ave. E. Exit. Turn east onto Sahara and go to Las Vegas Blvd. S. Turn south. The hotel-resort is visible on the west side of the road. Free parking on site. About 30 minutes from McCarran International Airport.

➛ By public transit, take city bus route 301.

**NEARBY**

➛ The Sahara, Guinness World of Records Museum and Gift Shop, Wet 'n Wild.

**COMMENT**

➛ Plan at least a 30-minute visit and for as long as 4 hours. The arcade area adjacent to the performers' ring has the latest hi-tech virtual-reality games.

## *Tricks of the Trade*

# INSTRUCTION IN THE PERFORMING ARTS

Have your kids have ever expressed an interest in taking formal lessons in dance, acting, voice or music? Consider enrolling them in classes at one of these establishments.

## Nevada Ballet Theatre

**1651 Inner Circle, Las Vegas**
**(702) 24DANCE (243-2623)**

Classes for children in ballet; jazz, ballroom and hip-hop dancing; acting; voice; piano; musical theater; fencing.

## Fern Adair Conservatory of the Arts

**3265 E. Patrick Lane, Las Vegas**
**(702) 458-7575**

Classes in ballet; jazz, tap and modern dancing; children's theatre; music.

## Academy of Dance and Performing Arts

**3755 E. Desert Inn Rd., Las Vegas**
**(702) 451-1666**

Classes in ballet, tap, jazz and musical theater.

# *More Culture for Kids*

## Annual Family Film Festival

**Jaycee Park, 2100 E. St. Louis Ave., Las Vegas**
**(702) 229-6211**

Sponsored by the City of Las Vegas, this festival runs for six consecutive Thursday evenings during mid-summer. Free admission. Call for a schedule of upcoming presentations.

## Las Vegas Youth Orchestra

**Sponsored by City of Las Vegas and the Clark County School District**
**(702) 384-8948**

Concerts for all ages in various venues. Call for dates, prices and locations.

## Rainbow Company Children's Theatre

**821 Las Vegas Blvd. N., Las Vegas**
**(702) 229-6553**

Features a lineup of stage productions for kids and their families. Call for a schedule of upcoming plays. General admission $5, teens and seniors $3, children (12 and under) $2. (Prices may vary depending on the play.)

CHAPTER 7

# ANIMALS, FARMS & ZOOS

# Introduction

Only in Las Vegas can families see spectacular lions and tigers, as well as sharks, penguins and other wild creatures amongst luxury hotels and top-notch restaurants.

Begin your animal encounter at the Lion Habitat at the MGM Grand. Your kids can get an up-close look at the denizens of the deep at the Shark Reef in Mandalay Bay. Don't forget to check out the white tigers at the Mirage. The Secret Garden of Siegfried & Roy, also at the Mirage, is home to many other large and rare felines. The Wildlife Habitat at the Flamingo, just a few blocks away, has a menagerie of wild animals that kids can ogle.

Las Vegas was a frontier town before the glitzonistas took over and that lingering influence shows up in old-time animal attractions. Make sure your animal-viewing itinerary includes the Gilcrease Bird Sanctuary and the Southern Nevada Zoological-Botanical Park, the only "true" zoos in the region.

Looking for something that's really untamed? The Henderson Bird Viewing Preserve is as natural as it gets. While the desert landscape doesn't support crops very well, the Henderson Farmer's Market and farmer's markets in Las Vegas give visitors a taste of the freshest products that the agricultural regions surrounding Nevada can offer.

**NOTE**

Kids can see more animals at these sites, described elsewhere in this guide:

Las Vegas Natural History Museum (Chapter 2, page 42)
Lake Mead National Recreation Area (Chapter 4, page 72)
Floyd Lamb State Park (Chapter 8, page 146)
Red Rock Canyon National Conservation Area (Chapter 8, page 150)
Spring Mountain Ranch State Park (Chapter 8, page 151)
Spring Mountains National Recreation Area (Chapter 8, page 153)

# *Flock to the* GILCREASE BIRD SANCTUARY

**8103 Racel St., Las Vegas**
**(702) 645-4224**

Here is another piece of the past; a fragment of the tourism Las Vegas relied on before it became the neon megalopolis. The Gilcrease Bird Sanctuary is unique. Its pens are handmade and look rustic compared to the streamlined exhibits of a modern zoo. But that just adds to its charm.

The sanctuary is very laid-back. If you bring your own bread, the kids can feed the hundreds of ducks, geese and swans that find permanent or temporary refuge in the large pond. If you don't have your own bread, you may find someone—perhaps a sanctuary volunteer—who will share theirs with you.

There are birds of every type, color and description. Many have nicknames on their cages, which is another indication that this is more than just a place that displays animals. Some of the feathered residents will greet visitors with a "hello." In other cases, the beauty of the birds—such as the spectacular blue and gold macaws—is enjoyment enough. For a true educational experience, be sure to point out the turkeys—Gilcrease has both wild and showy domestic ones. The sanctuary also has a nature trail, where visitors will find quaint aviaries created for Boy Scout projects.

#### SEASONS AND TIMES

➛ Year-round: Wed–Sun, 10 am–4 pm.

#### COST

➛ $3 per person.

#### GETTING THERE

➛ By car, take I-15 N. to U.S. 95 and continue north until the Durango Dr. Exit. Take Durango north to Racel St. and turn east. The sanctuary is on the south side of the street. Free parking on site. About 45 minutes from McCarran International Airport.

#### NEARBY

➛ Mount Charleston, Floyd Lamb State Park.

#### COMMENT

➛ Stop at Gilcrease before visiting Floyd Lamb State Park with its own complement of showy peacocks. Plan a 1-hour visit.

## *Developing Junior Birders*
# THE HENDERSON BIRD VIEWING PRESERVE

**2400-B Moser Dr., Henderson**
**(702) 566-2940**
**www.cityofhenderson.com/parks/parks.html**

Since the 1960s, bird lovers have visited the retention ponds at the City of Henderson's water-reclamation facility and kept tabs on a variety of birds that live there. By 1967, the ponds had become part of the local Audubon Society's annual Christmas Count because of shorebirds and migrating species. The seven large ponds do—believe it or not—constitute the third largest water body in the state, after Lake Mead and Lake Tahoe. In the late 1990s, the city decided to make the area an official bird-viewing site. They built paths and benches around the ponds and began augmenting the natural vegetation.

The landscaping will only get better with time, but the birds already seem satisfied. More than 200 species have been documented at the preserve, with about 11 new species being added each year. Placards make it easy to identify birds of particular interest, such as the roadrunner or the black-chinned hummingbird. The species checklist given to each party adds to the enjoyment. This is a great place for kids to run and play, with lots of open space and good protection from the ponds. But remember, these are wild animals that are not acclimatized to people and quickly flee when anyone ventures too close. Take your binoculars or purchase a pair in the preserve's gift shop. Make sure you have a good bird guide with you.

**SEASONS AND TIMES**

➛ Year-round: Daily, 6 am—3 pm.

**COST**

➛ Free.

**GETTING THERE**

➛ By car, take I-215 E. to I-515 N. and drive to the Sunset Rd. Exit. Head east on Sunset to Moser Dr., the 3rd street past the Boulder Hwy. intersection. Turn north on Moser to the preserve. Free parking on site. About 30 minutes from McCarran International Airport.

➛ By public transit, take city tour route 212.

**NEARBY**

➛ Clark County Heritage Museum, Henderson Farmer's Market.

**COMMENT**

➛ Go early in the morning for optimum viewing. Plan a 1- to 2-hour visit. For information on participating in the Christmas bird count, contact the Red Rock Audubon Society, the Las Vegas chapter of the National Audubon Society, at (702) 390-9890, or visit its website at www.communitylink.koz.com/lvrj/redrockaudubon

# *Fresh from the Farm*
# HENDERSON FARMER'S MARKET

**Water St., Henderson**
**(702) 565-2181**
**www.cityofhenderson.com/community/community.html**

Afraid your kids are going to grow up thinking that carrots and apples are harvested from a supermarket? Las Vegas can't help you with U-pick farms or farm tours, as very little produce grows in the desert. But kids can see the next best thing at the Henderson Farmer's Market. It is held every Thursday on Water Street in downtown Henderson (inside at the nearby convention center when temperatures reach an unbearable mark in summer). The market features every kind of fruit, vegetable and nut grown in the surrounding farming areas of California, Utah, Arizona and northern Nevada, where potatoes are grown.

It's also a good place to purchase wonderful whole-grain bread baked by a specialty bakery in Utah. Consider indulging in treats such as flavored soy nuts, roasted corn and sweet potatoes, funnel cakes, cotton candy and kettle corn—a type of sweetish popcorn that's cooked before your eyes. It's a welcome warm snack for a cold evening. Home-based businesses take advantage of the market to display their wares and you can purchase some handmade goods on the spot.

What's even better is that most of the people who work the stalls are especially receptive to kids, handing out the occasional free sample and special treats near Halloween. The fountains in the plaza of the adjacent Henderson Convention Center give kids something else to watch.

**SEASONS AND TIMES**

→ Summer (Apr—Oct): Thu, 4 pm—8 pm. Winter (Nov—Mar): Thu, 3 pm—7 pm.

**COST**

→ Free to browse.

**GETTING THERE**

→ By car, take I-215 E. to the end, where it becomes Lake Mead Blvd. Take Lake Mead east to Water St. (the last main intersection before Boulder Hwy.) and turn south. The farmer's market is farther down Water. Free parking on site. About 35 minutes from McCarran International Airport.

→ By public transit, take city bus route 216.

**NEARBY**

→ Clark County Heritage Museum, Lake Mead, Boulder City.

**COMMENT**

→ Consider stopping at the farmer's market either on your way to or from visiting Hoover Dam or the Boulder City-Hoover Dam Historical Museum.

**SIMILAR ATTRACTIONS**

These are the addresses for farmer's markets in Las Vegas; for more information about them, call (702) 562-2676.

→ **Village Square Shopping Center** · West Sahara Ave. at Fort Apache Rd. Year-round: Sun, 8 am—noon.

→ **Bruce Trent Park** · 1600 N. Rampart Blvd. Year-round: Wed, 2 pm—6 pm.

→ **Colonnade Square** · 8878 S. Eastern Ave. Year-round: Sat, 8 am—noon.

# *A Roar of Approval*
# LION HABITAT

**MGM Grand, 3799 Las Vegas Blvd. S., Las Vegas**
**(702) 891-1111**
**www.mgmgrand.com**

If you've ever been awed by the magnificent lion that roars at the beginning of every MGM movie, then you've got to make tracks to the luxurious lion habitat at the MGM Grand. Every day, this attraction features as many as five lions including Metro, Goldie and Baby Lion, who look like big pussycats. They nudge big plastic balls and other toys with their noses and parade around their fancy digs. And what digs they are, "furnished" with waterfalls, rock overhangs, trees and plants. Your backyard should look so good.

What's great about this place, in addition to the free admission, is the set-it-yourself pace. Kids can linger as long as they want, trying to catch the eye of one of the big beasts or waiting for a trainer to start playing with one of their charges. Glass walls and a see-through walkway offer protection for both lions and humans, while providing a good look at the fantastic felines. Depending on the time of your visit, kids may get their portrait shot while cuddling a lion cub. The gift shop, at the end of the self-guided walk-through tour, offers all sorts of souvenirs, books and pictures.

**SEASONS AND TIMES**

➛ Habitat: Year-round, daily, 11 am—11 pm. Gift shop: Year-round, daily, 9 am—11 pm.

**COST**

➛ Free.

**GETTING THERE**

➛ By car, take I-15 N. to the Tropicana Blvd. E. Exit. Head east on Tropicana. The hotel is on the northeast corner of the Las Vegas Blvd. intersection. Free parking on site. About 15 minutes from McCarran International Airport.

➛ By public transit, take city bus route 301.

**NEARBY**

➛ New York-New York, the Excalibur, the Luxor, M&M's™ World.

**COMMENT**

➛ During summer, consider combining the Habitat with an afternoon at the MGM Grand Adventure theme park or the roller coaster and arcade at New York-New York. In winter, include a stop at M&M's™ World. Plan a 30-minute visit.

*Animal Rarities*

# THE SECRET GARDEN OF SIEGFRIED & ROY

**The Mirage, 3400 Las Vegas Blvd., Las Vegas**
**(702) 791-7111**
**www.mirage.com**

Walking through Siegfried and Roy's animal collection, tucked behind the Mirage, really does feel like a visit to a secret garden. Plenty of animals live here and most are threatened or endangered. Siegfried and Roy have devoted themselves not only to magic, but also to help perpetuate some of the species nearing extinction. This may be the only chance kids have to see these animals and they likely won't forget the visit anytime soon.

On display are heterozygous white lions and tigers, so designated because they carry the genetic code for a white coat (necessary for the preservation of the Royal White Tigers of Nevada that the magicians have worked tirelessly to develop). The Secret Garden also has black panthers and striped white tigers, as well as snow leopards, snow white tigers and Asian elephants. There aren't any performances, but just watching the animals is always interesting.

And there's more. Your admission includes a tour of the 2.5 million-gallon Dolphin Habitat. The Atlantic bottlenose dolphins living here are transplants from other facilities or were born in Las Vegas. These marine mammals don't perform either, but visitors can see them frolicking in the water and interacting with their trainers.

**SEASONS AND TIMES**

➛ Secret Garden: Year-round, Mon, Tue, Thu and Fri, 11 am–5 pm; Sat–Sun, 10 am–5 pm. Dolphin Habitat: Mon–Fri, 11 am–7 pm; Sat–Sun, 10 am–7 pm.

**COST**

➛ Secret Garden and Dolphin Habitat: Individuals $10, under 11 free. Wednesdays when the Secret Garden is closed the Dolphin Habitat charges $5 per person, under 11 free.

**GETTING THERE**

➛ By car, take I-15 N. to the Flamingo Rd. E. Exit. Take Flamingo east to Las Vegas Blvd. S. and turn north. The Mirage will be the second resort on the west side of the street. Free parking on site. About 25 minutes from McCarran International Airport.

➛ By public transit, take city tour route 301.

**NEARBY**

➛ Treasure Island, the Venetian, Caesars Palace.

**COMMENT**

➛ Plan a 2- to 3-hour visit.

# *Creatures from the Deep*
# SHARK REEF

**Mandalay Bay, 3950 Las Vegas Blvd. S., Las Vegas**
**(702) 632-7777**
**www.mandalaybay.com**

It's billed as Shark Reef at Mandalay Bay, but it offers so much more. In fact, the attraction has nearly 2,000 animals comprising 100 different species that visitors can see during the audio tour. There are sharks, jellyfish, amphibians, reptiles and an assortment of bizarre-looking sea creatures. As visitors follow along, the tour leads them from one exhibit to the next, starting with golden crocodiles, then sea turtles, water monitors and lots of fish.

Particularly mesmerizing is a vertical tank filled with ethereally colored, translucent jellyfish, which seem to illuminate as they drift up and down. In another tank, visitors are challenged to spot moray eels that lay motionless between the rocks of their faux-sea environment. At the big pond area, kids can sit on the stone border and reach in and touch the horseshoe crabs and stingrays (it is safe since their stingers have been removed).

But the star of the show is the monstrous shark-reef exhibit. Its 1.3 million gallons of water are home to sharks of all shapes and sizes—ten varieties in all, including black-tip, bonnethead, sand tiger and nurse sharks. Kids have great fun dashing across the reef's glass floor and daring the fish below.

**SEASONS AND TIMES**

→ Year-round: Daily, 10 am—11 pm (last admission at 10 pm).

**COST**

→ Adults $13.95, children (5 to 12) $9.95, under 5 free.

**GETTING THERE**

→ By car, take I-15 N. to Tropicana Blvd. E. Head east on Tropicana to Las Vegas Blvd. S., and turn south. Mandalay Bay is the second resort on the west side of the road. Free parking on site. About 15 minutes from McCarran International Airport.

→ By public transit, take city bus route route 301.

**NEARBY**

→ New York-New York, MGM Grand, the Luxor.

**COMMENT**

→ Plan a 1- to 2-hour visit.

# *Migrating to the* SOUTHERN NEVADA ZOOLOGICAL-BOTANICAL PARK

**1775 N. Rancho Dr., Las Vegas**
**(702) 647-4685**
**www.lvrj.com/communitylink/zoo**

No doubt about it, the Southern Nevada Zoological-Botanical Park is a serious blast from the past; a zoo the way zoos used to be—modest, quaint and definitely low-tech. It's packed onto 2.5 acres in the middle of a residential area and encroached upon from all sides. And while not enjoying government funding or corporate support like many of its larger counterparts, the dedicated staff and devoted volunteers are doing their best to spiff the place up.

Among the many animals are Midas and Maniac Girl, the African lions born in 1998. The zoo also has swamp wallabies (including two joeys), a desert tortoise, beautiful brown-eyed mule deer, a chimpanzee, American alligators, a mountain lion and a Barbary ape. There are enough birds here to repopulate a good-sized forest, from ostriches and pheasants to golden eagles. Kids can run among the free-roaming roosters and chickens and spot fluffy chicks. In the reptile pavilion, they can see snakes and lizards from all over the world, including some native to southern Nevada.

It may not be the glitziest, but the zoo operators' hearts are in the right place. Some of the animals living here were rescued from owners who abandoned them. And a handmade memorial that reads "In Memory of Arnie, our Beloved African Lion, 1982-1997," speaks eloquently of the spirit of this place.

**SEASONS AND TIMES**

→ Year-round: Daily, 9 am—5 pm.

**COST**

→ Adults $5.95, seniors (62 and older) and children (2 to 12) $3.95, under 2 free.

**GETTING THERE**

→ By car, take I-15 N. to U.S. Hwy. 95 N. and drive to the Rancho Dr. Exit. Head north on Rancho for about 7 blocks. The zoo is on the west side of the road. Free parking on site. About 35 minutes from McCarran International Airport.

→ By public transit, take city bus route 106.

**NEARBY**

→ Nevada State Museum and Historical Society, Lied Discovery Children's Museum, Las Vegas Natural History Museum.

**COMMENT**

→ Plan a 1- to 2-hour visit.

# *The Cat's Meow*
# WHITE TIGER HABITAT

**The Mirage, 3400 Las Vegas Blvd. S., Las Vegas**
**(702) 791-7111**
**www.mirage.com**

Ever wonder what those white tigers do when they're not on stage performing in Siegfried and Roy's magic show? They laze around their specially built habitat inside the street entrance at the Mirage. The habitat possesses a decidedly Bengali air befitting the big cats' heritage. It is a majestic, towering white setting the cats blend into, reflecting the blue of the pond and the tigers' eyes. Visitors may stand as long as they want at the plate-glass window and watch these gorgeous animals prowl or have a snooze. The cats are continuously rotated in and out of the habitat. The tigers themselves are descendants of a breeding pair that a maharaja bequeathed to the United States in the 1950s. Today, there are only a few dozen of them left in the world.

The White Tiger Habitat is a quick stop, but right around the corner is the Mirage lobby that boasts a 53-foot-long saltwater aquarium behind the front desk. The aquarium contains more than 1,000 fish species that are tended by the hotel's staff of marine biologists. Just past it, in the main atrium of the resort, are masses of tropical plants. It all adds up to wide-eyed adventure—especially for kids who are first-time visitors.

**SEASONS AND TIMES**

→ Year-round: Daily, 24 hours a day.

**COST**

→ Free.

**GETTING THERE**

→ By car, take I-15 N. to the Flamingo Rd. E. Exit. Take Flamingo east to Las Vegas Blvd. S. and turn north. The Mirage is the second resort on the west side of the road. Free parking on site. About 25 minutes from McCarran International Airport.

→ By public transit, take city bus route 301.

**NEARBY**

→ The Secret Garden of Siegfried & Roy, Treasure Island, the Venetian, Caesars Palace.

**COMMENT**

→ Consider combining this with the Secret Garden of Siegfried & Roy or a stop next door at Treasure Island to watch the pirate battle. Plan a 30-minute visit.

## *Putting the Fun in Fauna*

# WILDLIFE HABITAT AT THE FLAMINGO

**3555 Las Vegas Blvd. S., Las Vegas**
**(702) 733-3111**
**www.lvflamingo.com**

Just when you think Las Vegas is unlikely to offer up any more surprises—one pops up. No way would the unknowing suspect that a 15-acre animal habitat was tucked around the venerable Flamingo resort on the Strip. Naturally they've got flamingos. But would you also believe African penguins in a special habitat with water chilled to their liking? There are Japanese koi, black swans, mute swans, black-necked swans, wood ducks, mandarin ducks and African crowned cranes, parading around their own special areas. Some of the animals can be viewed from the restaurants and elaborate tropical pool area of the Flamingo, with a broad concrete path connecting them.

As you wander along admiring the wildlife, you may happen upon a wedding in the gardens. There is also the memory of the wild life of Las Vegas' past tucked among the animals—a memorial to Bugsy Siegel, founder of the Flamingo.

**SEASONS AND TIMES**

→ Year-round: Daily, 24 hours a day.

**COST**

→ Free.

**GETTING THERE**

→ By car, take I-15 N. to the Flamingo Rd. E. Exit. Take Flamingo east to Las Vegas Blvd. and turn north. The Flamingo is the second resort on the east side of the street. Free parking on site. About 25 minutes from McCarran International Airport.

→ By public transit, take city bus route 301.

**NEARBY**

→ The Secret Garden of Siegfried & Roy, the Mirage, Treasure Island, the Venetian, Caesars Palace.

**COMMENT**

→ Consider combining with the White Tiger Habitat at the Mirage. Plan a 30-minute visit.

# CHAPTER 8

# GREEN SPACES

# Introduction

Green space in a desert sounds like an oxymoron. However, "Las Vegas" means "the meadows" in Spanish, and the springs that dot the region provide occasional patches of green.

Pack a lunch and take the gang for an afternoon at Floyd Lamb State Park or Spring Mountain Ranch State Park where grassy lawns, shade trees and picnicking lakeside will make you forget you are in the desert. Families never tire of visiting Lake Mead National Recreation Area, whether it is for a day or a couple of days of boating, swimming, hiking, camping and much more.

As you move into the mountains that ring the valley, the scrubby vegetation of the desert floor gives way to Joshua trees, pines, aspens and oak. You'll find options galore for fun in the fresh air. Spring Mountains National Recreation Area and Red Rock Canyon National Conservation Area boast trails for biking and hiking, stunning scenery and wildlife. Spring Mountains National Recreation Area also has skiing.

There are manmade green spaces throughout the metropolitan area, such as Sunset Park and Arroyo Grande Sports Complex in Henderson, where you can toss a ball or head to the playgrounds. Smaller parks, gardens and other green spots help make the valley more livable.

It all adds up to an oasis within an oasis. One thing to keep in mind though—this is the desert, and temperatures on mid-summer afternoons can climb well above 100 degrees in the sun. So take your sunscreen, wear a hat and pack plenty of water.

# *Hiking, Biking and Playing Ball*
# ARROYO GRANDE SPORTS COMPLEX

**298 Arroyo Grande, Henderson**
**(702) 565-4264**
**www.cityofhenderson.com/parks/parks.html**

The city of Henderson is known in Nevada for having the highest green-space-to-resident proportion in the state. Among the city's scattering of emeralds, the Arroyo Grande Sports Complex stands out as a 60-acre island of green in an otherwise brown desert landscape.

The complex offers everything a parkgoer could want: lighted youth baseball fields, adult softball fields, junior/adult baseball fields, basketball courts, announcing booths, playgrounds, snack bars, a covered picnic and barbecue area and restrooms. All are arrayed on a well-planned terraced layout and interconnected by a bike path/trail system. One of the playgrounds sits adjacent to the softball fields, so kiddies can play to their hearts' content while Mom and Dad take part in a game. Another plus is full access for people with disabilities.

Perched on a rise, the Arroyo Grande Sports Complex offers a breath-taking daytime view of the surrounding mountains. At night, the lights of the valley glitter like jewels, making the city sparkle.

**SEASONS AND TIMES**

➛ Year-round: Daily, 24 hours a day.

**COST**

➛ Free.

**GETTING THERE**

➛ By car, take I-215 E. to the Warm Springs Rd. Exit. Head east on Warm Springs to Arroyo Grande. Turn south and continue to the complex. It's on the east side of the road. Free parking on site. About 20 minutes from McCarran International Airport.

➛ By public transit, take city bus route 217.

**NEARBY**

➛ Galleria at Sunset shopping mall, Lake Mead National Recreation Area, Boulder City.

**COMMENT**

➛ This is a great place for organized activities or pack a picnic and just let the kids loose on the playground.

*Green Under Glass*

# BELLAGIO CONSERVATORY

**Bellagio, 3600 Las Vegas Blvd., Las Vegas**
**(702) 693-7111**
**www.bellagiolasvegas.com**

In the past few years, Las Vegas' Strip resorts have re-discovered the beauty that lush landscaping can add to their properties. Nowhere is this more evident than in the botanical garden at the luxe Bellagio.

The botanical garden, a glass-topped conservatory, is an escape to greenery for guests and visitors alike. The garden is filled with trees with the understory plantings—the flowers, small shrubbery and small accent plants—changing every season. A visitor is apt to find the place ablaze with bright yellow tulips in the spring (not unheard of in the desert, but certainly not common) and red and white poinsettias in the weeks surrounding Christmas. A 115-member staff is responsible for preparing and maintaining the 90,000-square-foot conservatory. It is supplied by a 30,000-square-foot greenhouse containing 8,000 potted plants, 500 shrubs and 32 full-size trees. Special lighting means that every blossom is shown to advantage—even after dark.

One caveat: children younger than 18 are not permitted inside the hotel unless they are registered guests or attending a hotel function (and then they must be at least five; strollers are only allowed for hotel guests). Families staying at the Bellagio, or taking in a performance of Cirque du Soleil's *O*, will find a visit to the conservatory well worth the detour.

**SEASONS AND TIMES**

→ Year-round: Daily, 24 hours a day.

**COST**

→ Free.

**GETTING THERE**

→ By car, take I-15 N. to the Flamingo Rd. E. Exit. Travel east on Flamingo to Las Vegas Blvd. and turn south. The hotel is on the west side of the boulevard. Free parking on site. About 10 minutes from McCarran International Airport.

→ By public transit, take city bus route 301.

**NEARBY**

→ The Aladdin, Caesars Palace, Flamingo.

**COMMENT**

→ If the age restriction is not an issue with your family, the conservatory is well worth the stop.

## *Paradise in the Sand*
# FLOYD LAMB STATE PARK

**9200 Tule Springs Rd., Las Vegas**
**(702) 486-5413**
**www.state.nv.us/stparks/fl.htm**

Floyd Lamb State Park is a peaceful, verdant escape from the hustle and bustle of the city and the brown bleakness of the desert landscape.

There are not many local spots, after all, where picnickers can relax on a broad lawn under towering trees while peacocks wander nearby. But this brilliant green spot has a past that may be surprising.

It started out conventionally enough. Tule Springs—where the park is located—was long known to natives as a good spot to stop for water. Prospectors also stopped at the oasis on their way north to try their luck in the mines. Visitors arriving in the 1940s and '50s were seeking a different kind of relief. By that time, Tule Springs had become a working ranch, and a change in divorce laws made Nevada's six-week residency requirement the shortest in the country. This brought five to six couples at a time to the ranch to ride horses, play tennis and relax around the pool and lakes while the clock ticked.

Today, a number of historic buildings from the Tule Springs Ranch (including an adobe hut dating to 1914-1918) survive in the park. The real draw is the lush surroundings. Visitors can fish, ride horses, hike, take wagon rides or just frolic on the lawn.

**SEASONS AND TIMES**

➛ Year-round: Daily, 9 am—dusk.

**COST**

➛ $5 per car.

**GETTING THERE**

➛ By car, take I-15 N. to US Hwy. 95 N. and drive to Durango Rd. Continue north to Tule Springs Rd. Follow Tule Springs northeast to the park. Free parking on site. About 45 minutes from McCarran International Airport.

**NEARBY**

➛ Mount Charleston, Indian Springs.

**COMMENT**

➛ Bring a picnic and spend the day. The park has pretty spots where you can lunch, many with scenic views of the lakes.

# *Meet Me at Mead*
# LAKE MEAD NATIONAL RECREATION AREA

**601 Nevada Hwy., Boulder City**
**(702) 293-8907 or (702) 293-8990**
**www.npa.gov/lame**

Here is a park your family will never tire of exploring. The Lake Mead National Recreation Area encompasses nearly 1.5 million acres along the Nevada-Arizona border, about 25 miles south of Las Vegas. It draws more than 9 million visitors each year.

The park offers a wealth of exploration possibilities for those interested in studying the desert. Three of the four desert ecosystems in the United States—Mohave, Great Basin and Sonora—are represented within its vast area.

Lake Mead (which was created when the Hoover Dam was built in the 1930s) and Lake Mohave are the main draws in this desert park. Boating, swimming, water-skiing and other water sports round out the picture.

Vacation cabins, resorts and campgrounds are available. For offbeat family fun, rent a houseboat and live on the lake for a few days—an experience that even the Strip hotels have been unable to match.

Not quite that brave? Consider renting a conventional boat for a few hours or letting the older kids take off on personal watercraft. One caveat: while water temperatures can reach 85 degrees during summer, they can dip to 45 degrees in winter.

**SEASONS AND TIMES**

➛ Park: Year-round, daily, 24 hours a day. Visitor center: Daily, 8:30 am–4:30 pm. Closed Thanksgiving, Christmas and New Year's.

**COST**

➛ $5 per vehicle. There are fees for rentals; call the park or visit its website for details.

**GETTING THERE**

➛ By car, take U.S. Hwy. 93 S. Continue south for about 24 miles until you see the signs for Lake Mead National Recreation Area. Free parking on site. About 45 minutes from McCarran International Airport.

➛ By public transit, no regular service exists. Grayline Las Vegas (800-634-6579), Quality Tours of Las Vegas (702-631-2292) and other tour bus companies make the run from Las Vegas.

**NEARBY**

➛ Hoover Dam (within the park), Boulder City, Arizona border.

**COMMENT**

➛ Definitely worth a stop for a few hours. Tell friends and relatives you tried water sports in the desert!

## *What's Your Pleasure?*

# RED ROCK CANYON NATIONAL CONSERVATION AREA

**State Rd. 159, Las Vegas**
**(702) 363-1921**
**www.nv.blm.gov/vegas/redrock/red2.htm**

Action-adventurers rock-climb in Red Rock Canyon National Conservation Area. Fitness fans in-line skate or bike the 13-mile scenic loop road through the canyon. Hikers stretch their legs over 30 miles of trails, some of which are easy enough for families to tackle together. If that sounds too strenuous, take the scenic drive in your car and enjoy the stunning views of red sandstone mixed with bands of white limestone.

Red Rock Canyon is a stunner. The 197,000-acre park is a super example of the Mohave Desert environment. Displays at the visitor center and interpretative talks by rangers help explain the ecosystem to visitors.

One popular interpretive program, Red Rock Art, takes hikers past three often-overlooked sites of petroglyphs, or prehistoric rock art. And there's more. The visitor center's annual fall Harvest Festival highlights cowboy poetry, Native American dancers, children's activities and craft demonstrations.

Whichever way you choose to see Red Rock Canyon, keep an eye out along the way. You might spot a wild burro or bighorn sheep!

**SEASONS AND TIMES**

➛ Scenic drive: Year-round, daily, 7 am–8 pm. Visitor center: Year-round, daily, 8:30 am–4:30 pm.

**COST**

➛ $5 per car. Fees for camping and some programs.

**GETTING THERE**

➛ By car, take I-15 N. to the Charleston Blvd. W. Exit. Head west on Charleston (State Rd. 159) to the Red Rock park entrance. Free parking on site. About 40 minutes from McCarran International Airport.

**NEARBY**

➛ Spring Mountain Ranch State Park.

**COMMENT**

➛ If time is short, take in the scenery by driving the loop road.

# *Poking Around* SPRING MOUNTAIN RANCH STATE PARK

**Blue Diamond Rd., Blue Diamond**
**(702) 875-4141**
**http://travelnevada.com/plan_visit/parks/parks_lasvegas.html#lasvegas**

The "Spring Mountain Ranch" part of this state park's name may sound as suspect as a jackalope, but it really is in the foothills of the mountains, there really are springs (52, to be exact) and it once was a working ranch.

Over the years it's been operated by a series of interesting owners—from pioneer mountain man Bill Williams and the Wilson family (who tamed the rugged area in the 19th century), Vera Krupp (owner of the Krupp Diamond, which Richard Burton later gave to Elizabeth Taylor) to Howard Hughes.

Today, it is a 528-acre state park with a spring-fed lake, a broad range of vegetation and an expanse of green lawn shaded by huge spreading trees. It is a fantastic setting for a picnic. Either before or after lunch visitors can tour the ranch house, built in 1948 by Chester Lauck of "Lum and Abner" radio fame. Kids will be fascinated by the bedroom added by Vera Krupp and accessed by a hidden hallway, its entrance disguised by a closet door.

The hilly terrain is a great way for kids to burn up excess energy—either by exploring on their own, or on one of the free guided tours around the property. A living-history program in which docents impersonate various personalities in the ranch's past is educational and entertaining for kids and parents alike.

**SEASONS AND TIMES**

➛ Ranch house: Year-round, daily, 10 am—4 pm. Picnic area: Year-round, daily, 8 am—dusk.

**COST**

➛ $5 per car.

**GETTING THERE**

➛ By car, take I-15 N. to the Charleston Blvd. W. Exit. Head west on Charleston (State Hwy. 159) to the park entrance. Free parking on site. About 40 minutes from McCarran International Airport.

**NEARBY**

➛ Red Rock Canyon National Conservation Area.

**COMMENT**

➛ Bring a ball to toss and a picnic lunch. Plan to spend the afternoon.

## *Doing the Charleston*

# SPRING MOUNTAINS NATIONAL RECREATION AREA

**2881 Valley View Blvd., Suite 16 (office), Las Vegas**
**(702) 873-8800**

Families who want to escape the oppressive heat of the Las Vegas Valley need only drive to Mount Charleston. About 35 miles northwest of town, it is 20 to 30 degrees cooler than the valley.

Mount Charleston is the popular local name for the 316,000-acre Spring Mountains National Recreation Area. Part of Toiyabe National Forest, 11,918-foot Charleston Peak (the third highest in Nevada) is its centerpiece.

The area boasts permanent and seasonal residents. The Mount Charleston Hotel and Mount Charleston Lodge offer food, drink, hotel rooms, cabin rentals and wedding facilities. There are no gasoline or grocery services on the mountain.

Recreational opportunities abound, many geared to families. In winter, ski or snowboard at the Las Vegas Ski and Snowboard Resort. In summer, camping, hiking and picnicking are popular. Hiking trails are well marked and include such points of interest as Cathedral Rock and Mary Jane Falls. The Desert View trail—a paved lane constructed for disabled visitors—is a gentle, easily accessible trail for all ages with sweeping views of the area, including the Nevada Test Site.

**SEASONS AND TIMES**

➛ Year-round: Daily, 24 hours a day. Establishments operating within the recreation area have their own hours.

**COST**

➛ Admission and trail use is free. Establishments operating within the recreation area charge fees.

**GETTING THERE**

➛ By car, take I-15 N. to U.S. Hwy. 95. Go north on 95 to State Rd. 156 or 157. Head west to the mountains. Free parking on site. About 45 minutes from McCarran International Airport.

**NEARBY**

➛ Floyd Lamb State Park, Indian Springs.

**COMMENT**

➛ The scenery and views are breathtaking. You will forget you are in Las Vegas. Plan to spend several hours.

# *Fun from Sunrise at Sunset*
# SUNSET PARK

**2601 E. Sunset Rd., Las Vegas**
**(702) 455-8200**
**www.co.clark.nv.us/parkrec/Parks.htm**

If you can't find something to do at Sunset Park, you aren't really trying. Laid out along a principal thoroughfare (Sunset Road), Sunset Park is not far from McCarran International Airport—one of the busiest airports in the country—and convenient to nearly everything in the area.

At any time during the day or night, the park attracts tennis, basketball and beach volleyball enthusiasts. Impromptu soccer games are likely to spring up. The park is also popular with in-line skaters, skateboarders and bikers who make their way along a network of pleasant trails and roadways.

Then there are the park's ball fields, fitness course, disc-golf course, horseshoe pits, radio-controlled boating, dog park and swimming pool. A community center is available for planned activities and there are picnic areas for planned or unplanned ones. The tree-shaded picnic grove is an especially inviting spot for neighborhood get-togethers.

If the park's many diversions don't prove to be sufficiently entertaining, you always can watch the jetliners lined up like constellations in the night sky as they await clearance to land.

**SEASONS AND TIMES**

➛ Year-round: Daily, 7 am—10 pm.

**COST**

➛ Free, except when using the pool.

**GETTING THERE**

➛ By car, take I-215 E. to the Sunset Rd. Exit. Go east on Sunset to the park. It is on the south side of the street. Free parking on site. About 10 minutes from McCarran International Airport.

➛ By public transit, take city bus route 212.

**NEARBY**

➛ McCarran International Airport, Liberace Museum.

**COMMENT**

➛ Pickup games are common in nearly every sport. Consider holding your child's next birthday in the park; there's nothing organized but you can set up your own.

CHAPTER 9

# HISTORICAL SITES

# Introduction

Many historical sites abound in Southern Nevada if you know where to look. Ghosts towns are a favorite and the region is dotted with them thanks to the boom-or-bust nature of mining communities that sprang up in the 19th century. Many of these ghost towns are best viewed from the car. The mine sites and old structures can be unstable and occasionally, explosives dumped long ago are discovered.

If you go exploring in the summer, carry plenty of water. The heat is not only oppressive; it can be downright dangerous. Wear plenty of sunscreen and let someone know where you are going and when you will be back.

Less hazardous historic sites for families also abound in the region. Take the gang to check out the artifacts at the Nevada State Museum and Historical Society, Lost City Museum and reconstructed Old Mormon Fort. There's Wild West fun at Bonnie Springs/Old Nevada. For recent history, the Boulder City Historic District offers visitors a feel of the 1930s.

**NOTE**

While Grapevine Canyon, Lost City Museum and Valley of Fire are more than an hour's drive from Las Vegas, they are too good to leave out. More history awaits families at these other attractions in this guide:

Boulder City-Hoover Dam Museum (Chapter 2, page 33)
The Clark County Heritage Museum (Chapter 2, page 35)
The Tomb and Museum of King Tutankhamun (Chapter 2, page 49)

# *Chasing Bad Guys at* BONNIE SPRINGS RANCH/OLD NEVADA

**Charleston Blvd., Las Vegas**
**(702) 875-4191**
**www.bonniesprings.com/oldnevada.html**

When you enter Bonnie Springs, the marshal may ask your kids to join a posse and flush out a bad guy barricaded in a building. Don't laugh too loud when the outlaw fires a shot and posse members drop to the ground. Things only get better. The good guys magically come back to life firing index-finger guns that cause signs, a thermometer and other things to fall off the building.

Such is the scene at Bonnie Springs—a lot of corn and a lot of fun. If you're expecting a polished attraction, this isn't it. But Bonnie Springs has learned to make fun of itself. The melodrama features an actor who repeatedly changes from one cheesy wig to the next, and sound effects that tend to be a little off. Kids eat up the action. Parents will laugh at the outhouse humor and double entendres that sail over the little ones' heads.

The wax museum is not Madame Tussaud's, but it works in quite a bit of Nevada history, as does the antique stamp mill. After all, this is a true historic site. Bonnie Springs Ranch was built in 1843 as a stopover for wagon trains en route to California.

Other on-site attractions include a hotel, wedding chapel, cactus garden, restaurant, horseback riding and train rides. The petting zoo is a little cramped, but where else can kids experience the thrill of mingling with deer?

**SEASONS AND TIMES**

→ Year-round: Daily, 10:30 am–5 pm.

**COST**

→ Adults $6.50, children (5 to 11) $4, under 5 free.

**GETTING THERE**

→ By car, take I-215 W. to I-15 and head south to the Blue Diamond Rd. Exit. Go west on Blue Diamond (State Rd. 160) to State Rd. 159 and travel north toward the Red Rock Canyon area. Bonnie Springs is about 8 miles up the road on the west side. Free parking on site. About 35 minutes from McCarran International Airport.

**NEARBY**

→ Spring Mountain Ranch State Park, Red Rock Canyon National Conservation Area.

**COMMENT**

→ Plan at least a 3-hour visit.

# *Strolling through Yesteryear*
# BOULDER CITY HISTORIC DISTRICT

**Bounded by Nevada Hwy., Avenue L, Date and Fifth streets, Boulder City**
**(702) 293-2034 (Chamber of Commerce)**
**www.bouldercity.com**

Boulder City is a vibrant, growing community with new subdivisions and booming businesses. It's also the only place in Nevada where gambling is illegal.

History reigns supreme at Boulder City. It was created in the 1930s to house workers building Hoover Dam (page 92). And to this day, the dam still casts a broad shadow over the town. History Central is the quaint little district along the Nevada Highway.

This pleasant stretch of road features galleries, antique shops, a doll shop and a Native jewelry store and is perfect for a stroll with the family. Stop at any of the establishments and browse as long as you like. At mealtime, the Happy Days drive-in and Coffee Cup coffee shop offer visitors a blast from the past—maybe not the '30s, but certainly the'50s.

The old Boulder City Hotel near the west end of the district houses the Boulder City-Hoover Dam Museum (page 33). You'll find art galleries and gift shops in the area as well. At the east end, sharp-eyed visitors will spot the quaint brick-and-tile houses built for the officials managing the dam project. The nearby Bicentennial Park is a seven-acre expanse of green with towering trees and—a little incongruously—a big piece of machinery from the dam. The park's play area brings kids quickly back to the present.

**SEASONS AND TIMES**

➛Year-round: Hours vary by business.

**COST**

➛ Free.

**GETTING THERE**

➛ By car, take I-515 and U.S. Hwy. 93 S. to Boulder City. Skip the bypass and follow Nevada Hwy. into town. Shortly after the 93 fork, turn north onto Ash St. and then east onto Arizona St. Free parking on site. About 45 minutes from McCarran International Airport.

➛ By public transit, take city bus route 107 to Racetrack Rd. Transfer to route 116 to Boulder City.

**NEARBY**

➛ Hoover Dam, Lake Mead National Recreation Area.

**COMMENT**

➛ Plan a 1-hour walking tour; longer with stops.

# *Hitting Pay Dirt*
# EL DORADO MINES

**State Rd. 165, Nelson**

Nelson is a "living" ghost town. Few residents and even fewer businesses remain in Greater Nelson, whose glory days faded with the end of the El Dorado mines.

The appearance of Europeans here was earlier than in most parts of Southern Nevada. The Spanish made the initial discovery of gold in the area in 1775 and named it El Dorado Canyon. It was a century later that mining began in earnest.

Millions of dollars in gold, silver, copper and lead came out of the El Dorado mines during its heyday from 1885 through to the mid-'40s. With so much at stake—realistically and in the dreams of the miners—tempers flared regularly and the area became notorious for its violence. Many of the 500 miners who worked the area are said to have been Civil War deserters.

Today there are abandoned mines along the road in Nelson with modern homes in Nelson proper. Past Nelson, the road heads back to the north where visitors can enter the Lake Mead National Recreation Area (page 72). Continue on the road for a spectacular view of the Colorado River. An old historical marker at the intersection of U.S. 95 and State Road 165 tells a bit of the history of the area. Stop and read, and then enjoy a drive-through, imagine things as they were when this earth yielded one of the richest treasures known to man.

**SEASONS AND TIMES**

➛ Year-round: Daily, 24 hours a day.

**COST**

➛ Free.

**GETTING THERE**

➛ By car, take I-215 E. to its end and follow Lake Mead Dr. east to I-515/U.S. 93/U.S. 95 and head south on the combined highway. Continue south at the U.S. 95 turnoff just before Boulder City. Follow U.S. 95 for about 10 miles, and turn east on State Rd. 165. There will be a parking area and El Dorado Canyon marker at the intersection. Follow State Rd. 165 east to see Nelson. About 60 minutes from McCarran International Airport.

**NEARBY**

➛ Laughlin, Grapevine Canyon.

**COMMENT**

➛ Be sure to take plenty of sunscreen and water during the summer. Be mindful of hazards such as rattlesnakes, sidewinders, and the possibility of open mines and ventilation shafts. Plan a 1-hour visit.

# *Off the Beaten Path*
# GRAPEVINE CANYON

**Off State Rd. 163, near Laughlin**
**(800) 452-8445**

The road to Grapevine Canyon isn't an easy one, but it is rewarding. The canyon is a 90-mile drive from Las Vegas. Follow the gravel road through Christmas Tree Pass named for the junipers and pinyons at the upper elevations. At holiday time, many are decorated. A half-mile walk through the canyon brings you to walls bearing petroglyphs. Native people (believed to be the Yuman) living in this region in ancient times left these markings, some of which—such as bighorn sheep—are easily decipherable. You can see more petroglyphs in Valley of Fire State Park (page 173). Let the kids run off some energy, but don't let them touch the pictographs—they are fragile and priceless.

It's silent here, or nearly so. The only intrusions are the sounds of birds and the desert breeze. If you don't have small children, climb the surrounding ridges for a spectacular view of the Colorado River. Continuing along the gravel road through Christmas Tree Pass returns you to State Road 95. Visit Spirit Mountain along the way. The Mojave people considered it to be the center of the universe. Once you're back in civilization, you may understand why.

**SEASONS AND TIMES**

➛ Year-round: Daily, dawn—dusk. Laughlin Visitors Center: 8 am—4:30 pm.

**COST**

➛ Free.

**GETTING THERE**

➛ By car, take I-215 E. until it becomes Lake Mead Dr. Follow Lake Mead east to the I-515/U.S. 93/U.S. 95 interchange. Take the combined highway south to where U.S. 95 splits off (before Boulder City) and head south on 95 through Searchlight. Just south of Searchlight, take the State Rd. 163/Laughlin cutoff and head east. About 13 miles from the intersection, watch for the Christmas Tree Pass/Laughlin turnoff and head north on the gravel road. This 16-mile loop road will pass a short cutoff road to the Grapevine Canyon parking area. It re-connects with U.S. 95 just south of Searchlight. Free parking on site. About 90 minutes from McCarran International Airport.

**NEARBY**

➛ Laughlin, Nelson.

**COMMENT**

➛ Do not let small children scramble on the rocks; they can be dangerous. Stay alert for rattlesnakes and sidewinders. The National Park Service as part of the Lake Mead National Recreation Area administers the area. It is untamed wilderness with no amenities. Plan a 1-hour visit.

# *Finding Your Way to* LOST CITY MUSEUM

**721 S. Moapa Valley Blvd., Overton**
**(702) 397-2193**
**http://dmla.clan.lib.nv.us/docs/museums/lost/lostcity.htm**

So you think your kid's room is a pit? The Lost City Museum features a whole house that's a pit. The Basketmakers occupied the pit house during the Anasazi (Ancient Ones) period in southern Nevada. The ancient dwelling is one of several reconstructed Anasazi-era structures outside the museum.

The name of the museum commemorates the Pueblo Grande de Nevada, a 30-mile-long series of adobe ruins. This one-time vibrant and sprawling settlement had its heyday around 800 AD. During the visit, you'll learn about the Basketmakers, considered the forebearers of this civilization who lived here from about 300 BC to 700 AD. You also learn about the Anasazi civilization, which disappeared around 1150 AD due to prolonged drought.

Originally, the museum was built on the site of some of the pueblos. Later, a wing was added around the ruins so modern visitors could get an idea of how the pueblo was designed. There's no touching the displays inside the museum, but outside kids can enter some of the buildings to get a feel for the cramped surroundings from which the Anasazis built their advanced society.

You will experience a double layer of history. In 1935 members of the Civilian Conservation Corps (CCC), formed during the Great Depression, excavated the pueblo foundation and constructed the pit house. It is therefore fitting the museum display a CCC camp kit. Most of the displays in the museum will be of interest to kids of school age, but even tots will get some insight into the very different way of life of the region's first residents.

**SEASONS AND TIMES**

→ Year-round: Daily, 8:30 am—4:30 pm. Closed Thanksgiving, Christmas and New Year's.

**COST**

→ Individuals (18 and older) $2, under 18 free.

**GETTING THERE**

→ By car, take I-15 N. to Exit 93. Head southeast on State Rd. 169 through Logandale to Overton (about 12 miles). The museum is on the west side of the road, just past the center of Overton. Free parking on site. About 70 minutes from McCarran International Airport.

**NEARBY**

→ Valley of Fire State Park, Mesquite.

**COMMENT**

→ Bring a picnic lunch and enjoy the view from the museum grounds. Plan at least a 1-hour visit.

*History on Display*

# NEVADA STATE MUSEUM AND HISTORICAL SOCIETY

**700 Twin Lakes Dr. (in Lorenzi Park), Las Vegas**
**(702) 486-5205**
**http://dmla.clan.lib.nv.us/docs/museums/lv/vegas.htm**

Some 30 fossils of prehistoric Ichthyosaurs have been found in central Nevada. An easy way to learn about the big marine reptiles is to visit the Nevada State Museum and Historical Society. It has a full-size casting of an Ichthyosaur fossil. And what a size it is—48 feet long and 16 feet high. No wonder it is Nevada's official state fossil.

But it's not the only one. There's also a skeleton of a Columbian mammoth. The sheer size of the artifacts will awe kids. They will also like the museum's hands-on aspects. They can feel the ridges of a mammoth's upper tooth (mounted at kid level!) and do rubbings of smaller depictions of the mammoth and a Pacific horse.

At another interactive display, children choose the clothing that reflects a specific era, and then dress paper-doll-like figures. Adults are interested in listening to a recording in which an attorney recounts a conversation with Benjamin "Bugsy" Siegel, the notorious father of modern Las Vegas.

Siegel gives a chilling warning that seems to portend his own demise.

Other exhibits depict Nevada's living folk art and highlight Las Vegas' cultural diversity. Part of the state's history is also showcased in displays on mining, atomic testing and magnesium production. Inquire about the museum's programs. They include workshops for children and adults.

#### SEASONS AND TIMES

→ Year-round: Daily, 9 am—5 pm. Closed Thanksgiving, Christmas and New Year's.

#### COST

→ Adults $2, under 18 and museum members free.

#### GETTING THERE

→ By car, take I-15 N. to U.S. 95, head northwest on 95 to the Rancho Dr. Exit. Go north on Rancho to Washington Ave. and turn west. Drive passed Lorenzi Park to Twin Lakes Dr. and turn south. The museum is on the east side of the street. Free parking on site. About 30 minutes from McCarran International Airport.
By public transit, take city bus route 208.

#### NEARBY

→ Las Vegas Natural History Museum, Lied Discovery Children's Museum, Old Las Vegas Mormon Fort State Historic Park.

#### COMMENT

→ Plan at least a 1-hour visit.

## *Discovering Las Vegas' Roots*

# OLD LAS VEGAS MORMON FORT STATE HISTORIC PARK

**500 E. Washington Ave., Las Vegas**
**(702) 486-3511**
**www.state.nv.us/stparks/olvmf.htm**

Believe it or not, this humble fort is the birthplace of modern Las Vegas. The Old Las Vegas Mormon Fort State Historic Park is where 30 Mormon missionaries from Utah established a settlement in 1855. Until then, Las Vegas was but a watering spot on the Old Spanish Trail to California. The settlement lasted only a few years, but the legacy of those Mormon pioneers lives on in the city today.

A remnant of the original 150-square-foot fort—part of the old adobe building closest to the creek—remains intact. The rest of the structure has been re-constructed, so today's visitors can feel what it was like to be in the original pioneer group.

The little building with a sloping floor and low ceiling is furnished with an ancient sofa, chairs with animal-hide weaving and such old-time necessities as a spinning wheel and carding boards. Also view the Southern Paiute Native artifacts, cotton raised in Las Vegas and a photo of the old fort in 1905.

Best of all, the fort is a great spot for kids. They may get a little restless in the old building, but the grounds have plenty of wide-open space to run. A rustic ladder that leads to a tower lookout is suitable for all but the littlest. Kids will think it's cool to peer at the city below. Those 19th-century Mormon missionaries would no doubt agree.

**SEASONS AND TIMES**

➛ Year-round: Daily, 8 am—4:30 pm. Closed Christmas through New Year's.

**COST**

➛ Adults $2, children (6 to 12) $1, under 6 free.

**GETTING THERE**

➛ By car, take I-15 N. to I-515/U.S. 93/U.S. 95 S. Head south to the Las Vegas Blvd. Exit. Drive north on Las Vegas; the fort is on the east side of the road at the intersection of Washington Ave. Free parking on site. About 40 minutes from McCarran International Airport.

➛ By public transit, take city bus route 113.

**NEARBY**

➛ Las Vegas Natural History Museum, Cashman Center & Field, Lied Discovery Children's Museum.

**COMMENT**

➛ Plan at least a 30-minute visit. Consider combining this with the Las Vegas Natural History Museum, Lied Discovery Children's Museum or a special event at Cashman Center.

# *Deciphering Ancient Symbols at* VALLEY OF FIRE STATE PARK

**Off I-15, near Overton**
**(702) 397-2088**
**www.state.nv.us/stparks/vf.htm**

Be sure you are wearing comfortable walking shoes before venturing through the Valley of Fire. Staying on the road that circles this scenic state park, Nevada's oldest, means you'll miss the best it has to offer. The visitors center has maps and interpretive displays on the geology, ecology, prehistory and history of the park and surrounding region.

One of the park's most spectacular features is the Petroglyph Canyon trail. The self-guided tour takes you through a sandy canyon that's lined with examples of petroglyphs created by the Anasazis (Ancient Ones) who occupied the area from 300 BC to 1150 AD. The ancient writings are pictographs, and anyone with an imagination can get an idea of what the writers were saying. Keys lend further insight into their meaning.

Another not-to-be-missed attraction is Atlatl Rock, also featuring ancient writings. You'll have to climb a metal staircase to see them as they are high up a cliff. One of the symbols depicts an atlatl—a notched stick the ancients used to power spears faster and farther. Elsewhere you can see petrified wood—miles from any forest.

Don't miss Mouse's Tank. This bowl-shaped rock formation collects and stores the scant rainwater that falls in the desert. Mouse's Tank was named for a fugitive Paiute Native who hid out here in the 1890s. You have to scramble up a gentle slope to see it. The Beehives is another fascinating formation to behold, obviously named for its appearance.

**SEASONS AND TIMES**

→ Year-round: Daily, dawn—dusk. Visitors center: 8:30 am—4:30 pm.

**COST**

→ Entrance fee: $5 per vehicle per day. Other fees for camping and group use.

**GETTING THERE**

→ By car, take I-15 N. to Exit 75. Head west following the road to the park entrance. Free parking on site. About 70 minutes from McCarran International Airport.

**NEARBY**

→ Lost City Museum, Mesquite.

**COMMENT**

→ Plan at least a 3-hour visit.

CHAPTER 10

# GETTING THERE IS HALF THE FUN

# *Introduction*

It's been said that getting there is half the fun, and that's certainly true in Las Vegas. Often it means getting there by taking one of the monorails on the Strip, or one of the trolleys or buses that serve much of the area.

Sometimes it means enjoying the transportation as an experience in itself. Take a cruise on Lake Mead, float along an indoor canal on a gondola at The Venetian or trail ride at Sandy Valley Ranch by crisscrossing a valley that is the Old West.

Then there's just looking at modes of transportation by touring the auto collection at the Imperial Palace or parking near the airport to watch planes land and take off. There's even a fantasy transportation spot—the Race for Atlantis at Caesars. And what could be better—each offers plenty of fun for families to enjoy together.

# *Fine Set of Wheels*
# ANTIQUE AND CLASSIC AUTO COLLECTION

**Imperial Palace, 3535 Las Vegas Blvd. S., Las Vegas**
**(702) 731-3311**
**www.autocollections.com**

A bunch of cars in a great big room may not sound like much to anyone who isn't a dyed-in-the-wool car lover, but the Antique and Classic Auto Collection at the Imperial Palace holds more than a few surprises. You think today's SUV's are large? After seeing the huge Duesenbergs, you'll soon understand how the expression "it's a doozy" was coined. There are about 350 vehicles in the collection and nearly all are for sale. The price tags on the Duesenbergs are more than $1 million each.

Kids will enjoy seeing the 1982 Range Rover "Popemobile" with its domed top, the 1959 Cadillac Eldorado with fins stretching to eternity and the 1998 Corvette Indy Pace Car. Boomer parents can reminisce in front of the 1966 Volkswagen Sundial camper, complete with pup tent and wood-and-leather interior. Among the most fantastic exhibits are the 1979 Rolls Royce Silver Wraith armed with gun ports and oil and tear-gas systems, and the 1933 Lincoln KB Willoughby Panel Brougham. This "fine lady's coach" comes with sterling silver vanity case, smoking set, hassocks, throw pillows and an inter-compartment telephone.

Most of the cars can't be touched, but there is one exception. For the ultimate vicarious experience, load the kids into the old Ford for a unique family snapshot.

**SEASONS AND TIMES**

➛ Year-round: Daily, 9:30 am—11:30 pm.

**COST**

➛ Adults $6.95, seniors and children (under 13) $3. Visit the website and print out a pass for free admission.

**GETTING THERE**

➛ By car, take I-15 N. to the Flamingo Rd. Exit. Head east on Flamingo to Las Vegas Blvd. S. Turn north and drive to the entrance of the Imperial Palace. Free parking on site. About 20 to 30 minutes from McCarran International Airport.

➛ By public transit, take city bus route 301.

**NEARBY**

➛ The Bellagio, Caesars Palace, the Flamingo.

**COMMENT**

➛ Plan a 2-hour visit.

# *Going Public*
# CAT BUSES

**600 S. Grand Central Pkwy., Las Vegas**
**(702) 228-7433**
**www.rtc.co.clark.nv.us/cat/cat.htm**

Trying to get from here to there? You can—all through the Las Vegas Valley—on Citizens Area Transit (CAT) buses.

CAT operates 49 scheduled routes in Las Vegas, North Las Vegas, Henderson, Boulder City and the outlying areas of Laughlin, Mesquite and Virgin Valley. CAT buses are clean, comfortable and on schedule. They also come in several sizes from scaled-down to tandem, ensuring the biggest vehicles serve the busiest routes.

In most cases, full fare is $1.25 (exceptions are the Strip routes). Reduced fares are available for youths, seniors and riders with disabilities (reduced-fare ID cards must be secured in advance). Transfers are free and passengers may transfer twice to complete a one-way trip within two hours. It is therefore theoretically possible to get from North Las Vegas to Boulder City on one fare, provided there's no traffic.

Bear in mind, CAT is great for non-utilitarian transportation. It doesn't serve the most scenic areas of the county, such as Red Rock Canyon and Hoover Dam, but the bus can be a fun way for kids to see the sights.

**SEASONS AND TIMES**

➛ Year-round: Daily. Residential routes run from 5:30 am to 1:30 am. Other routes run 24 hours. Call CAT or visit its website for details.

**COST**

➛ On most routes riders older than 18 pay $1.25 ($2 on routes 301, 302 and 303). Seniors (62 and older) and youths (6 to 17) with reduced-fare card $0.60. Reduced-fare tokens and passes available at the Downtown Transportation Center (300 N. Casino Center Dr.). Kids under 6 ride free.

## *O Solo Mio*
# GRAND CANAL GONDOLA RIDE

**The Venetian, 3355 Las Vegas Blvd. S., Las Vegas**
**(702) 414-4500**
**www.venetian.com**

Sit back and listen to the gondolier sing as you float along and you'll swear you're in Venice. OK, so the canal is on the second floor and the water is chlorinated—use your imagination.

The shiny black gondolas were imported from Italy, as were some of the gondoliers. There's a lot that can be said for the novelty of gliding along in a gondola in Las Vegas. The ride is relaxing and the gondoliers are trained singers.

There are pauses every few minutes during the 20-minute ride. The Venetian-style arched bridges that traverse the canal are only high and wide enough for one gondola to pass at a time. The gondoliers take advantage of these pauses to burst into song—generally Italian opera, but sometimes Italian love songs.

This is a prime place for weddings, and kids have fun scoping out the brides and grooms. Weddings, sometimes several a day, take place on the bridges or on a special white gondola. Even without the wedding action, there's a lot to see—from the shops that line the canal to the shoppers treading the walkway between the canal and the stores.

**SEASONS AND TIMES**

➛ Year-round: Sun—Thu, 10 am—11 pm; Fri—Sat, 10 am—midnight.

**COST**

➛ $10 per person.

**GETTING THERE**

➛ By car, take I-15 N. to the Spring Mountain Rd. Exit. Head east on Spring Mountain to Las Vegas Blvd. S. Turn south on Las Vegas and drive to the entrance of The Venetian. Free parking on site. About 25 minutes from McCarran International Airport.

➛ By public transit, take city bus route 301.

**NEARBY**

➛ Harrah's, The Mirage, Treasure Island.

**COMMENT**

➛ Rarely is it possible to ride the gondola right away. Plan to arrive a few hours early, purchase your tickets and spend the intervening period exploring the Grand Canal Shops or Madame Tussaud's Celebrity Encounter. The gondolas seat four, which is ideal for most families. Smaller parties are sometimes seated with others. Plan at least a 1-hour visit.

## *Ahoy, Matey!*
# LAKE MEAD CRUISES

**Lakeshore Rd. (Hwy. 166), Lake Mead National Recreation Area, Boulder City**
**(702) 293-6180**
**www.lakemeadcruises.com**

The tour narration provided on Lake Mead Cruises may be pre-recorded and a little tinny, but the scenery is the real McCoy.

Lake Mead didn't exist until the 1930s, when Black Canyon was flooded after the construction of Hoover Dam (page 92). There are 70 million years of history, and the narrator traces much of it—from the Anasazi period, through the period when the Paiutes ruled the area, to the present day.

Younger kids may tire of the narration, but not of the dam and being on a boat cruising the big lake. Bighorn sheep can often be seen on the canyon's cliffs as the vessel heads into a narrow passage that brings passengers up close to the reverse of the dam face. It may not be Niagara Falls, but it's still a thrill for young and old alike.

### SEASONS AND TIMES

➛ Year-round: Times vary. Call for details. Options include breakfast buffet, midday excursion, dinner and dinner-dance cruises.

**COST**

➛ Midday excursion: Adults $18, children (under 12) $9. Early dinner cruise: Adults $35, children (under 12) $18. Dinner-dance cruise: Adults $49. Children younger than 2 cruise free.

**GETTING THERE**

➛ By car, take I-215 E. until it ends and becomes Lake Mead Dr. Head east on Lake Mead to I-515/U.S. 93/U.S. 95 and head south. Follow U.S. 93 southeast (after 515 ends and 95 turns off) through the second traffic light in Boulder City. Turn north onto Lakeshore Rd. The entrance to Lake Mead Cruises is about 3 1/2 miles down the road on the east side, past the entrance to Lake Mead National Recreation Area. Free parking on site. About 45 minutes from McCarran International Airport.

**NEARBY**

➛ Hoover Dam, Boulder City, Lake Mead National Recreation Area.

**COMMENT**

➛ The boat has secure railings, but it is wise to keep a sharp eye on little ones. Plan at least a 3-hour visit.

# *Take a Trip on* LAS VEGAS STRIP TROLLEYS

**The Strip and Downtown, Las Vegas**
**(702) 382-1404**

Looking for a fun way to see the city and avoid the downtown traffic? Hop aboard a Las Vegas street trolley.

The trolleys serving Las Vegas are not exactly authentic. They run on tires instead of rails, and you won't hear any clanging bells, but they still have an old-timey feel. They follow two routes, one traveling downtown between the Plaza Hotel on Main Street and the Stratosphere (page 22) on the north part of Las Vegas Boulevard South, the other along the Strip. If you want to see the whole shebang, get off one trolley at the Stratosphere and board the other. The hotel-casino is a common stop on the two routes, although you'll need to pay separate fares for each.

The Strip trolley runs from the Stratosphere down to the Luxor, one of the southernmost casinos on Las Vegas Boulevard South. It stops at the front door of each major property, even zagging over to the Las Vegas Hilton on Paradise Road, which runs parallel to the Strip.

During major conventions, events such as the National Finals Rodeo, or on busy holiday weekends, the trolleys may be packed during peak hours. If your schedule is flexible, ride the trolley early in the morning or late in the evening and avoid the crowds. Sit back and enjoy the sights.

#### SEASONS AND TIMES

➛ Year-round: Daily. Both trolleys run about every 15 minutes from 9:30 am to 1:30 am.

#### COST

➛ $1.50 per person. Exact change required.

#### GETTING THERE

➛ By car, to reach the Stratosphere, take I-15 N. to Sahara Ave. W. Head west on Sahara to Las Vegas Blvd. S. and turn north. The Stratosphere will be the first major property on the west side of the road. Free parking on site. About 30 minutes from McCarran International Airport.

➛ By public transit, take city bus route 301 to the Stratosphere.

**NEARBY**

➛ The downtown trolley runs close to the Fremont Street Experience and every major casino-hotel. On the Strip route the entire Las Vegas Blvd. is at your disposal.

**COMMENT**

➛ Some trolleys can be chilly on blustery evenings so bring a sweater.

*Take a Free Ride*

# MONORAILS ALONG THE STRIP

**Various terminuses along Las Vegas Blvd., Las Vegas**

All kids complain about the walk along the Strip. Here's a solution known only to locals and the most experienced visitor: cover the distance using the free monorails that run between the hotels. Most of them are sleek, modern-looking vehicles, gliding quietly between the resorts on elevated tracks.

The shortest leg is a hop between Treasure Island (page 24) and the Mirage (page 25). If you disembark there, it's a bit of a haul to the Bellagio (page 27). The monorail there goes to the Monte Carlo, several properties away. (Be mindful that kids under 18 aren't exactly welcome at the Bellagio unless you have rooms or dinner or show reservations).

Farther south on the same (west) side of the Strip is one of the more visible monorails—one that's closer to the street (most of the others are tucked away behind the resorts). It connects the Excalibur (page 28), Luxor (page 49) and Mandalay Bay (page 134).

Cross to the east side of the Strip to the longest of the Strip monorails, a streamlined, space-age vehicle that connects the MGM Grand (page 76) to Bally's, passing along the backs of the Aladdin and Paris, although it doesn't stop at those properties. This leg eventually will extend north past the Las Vegas Convention Center and possibly downtown.

**SEASONS AND TIMES**

→ Year-round: Daily, time vary. Call individual hotels for information.

**COST**

→ Free.

**GETTING THERE**

→ By car, take I-15 N. to any of the cross streets leading to the Strip properties mentioned above; all line Las Vegas Blvd. S. Parking is available at each property. About 25 minutes from McCarran International Airport.

→ By public transit, take city bus route 301.

**NEARBY**

→ All of the offerings on the Strip.

**COMMENT**

→ You'll need to walk between the terminuses. It is fun to see how far you can travel on the monorails and view the interesting stops along the way.

## A *Virtual Ride*
# RACE FOR ATLANTIS

**Forum Shops at Caesars, 3500 Las Vegas Blvd. S.,
Las Vegas
(702) 733-9000
www.caesars.com**

Here's a ride you won't soon forget—a flight into fantasy within the fantasy world of Caesars Palace.

The Race for Atlantis is actually located in the Forum Shops at Caesars, a luxury shopping area adjacent to Caesars Palace Hotel & Casino. The magic starts as soon as visitors approach the attraction's entrance near the Neptune Fountain. Kids are given paper crowns evocative of Caesar as they start the trek through the faux-stone hallways to the Race for Atlantis staging area.

Here the fantasy continues. The staging area—a winding, twisting walkway in a sort of mythical forest—is shrouded in mist and lit by linear colored lights. Then it's into a pre-show area. Visitors get their 3-D goggles and watch a video explaining the rules. The plot has passengers riding in a chariot to save the lost city of Atlantis from the ghastly Ghastlius. There's lots of virtual-reality soaring and zooming including a number of maneuvers through tight archways. It's a little rattling but not as much as most virtual-reality rides. The fantastic audio-visual special effects make this trip worth taking.

**SEASONS AND TIMES**

➛ Year-round: Sun—Thu, 10 am—11 pm; Fri—Sat, 10 am—midnight.

**COST**

➛ Adults $10 ($9 for Nevada residents), children (under 13) $7.

**GETTING THERE**

➛ By car, take I-15 N. to the Flamingo Rd. Exit. Head east on Flamingo to Las Vegas Blvd. S. Turn north on Las Vegas and drive to the entrance of Caesars Palace. Free parking on site. About 20 to 30 minutes from McCarran International Airport.

➛ By public transit, take city bus route 301.

**NEARBY**

➛ The Flamingo, Bellagio, Paris, Bally's.

**COMMENT**

➛ Riders must be at least 42 inches tall. Plan a 30-minute visit. Combine your ride with browsing the Forum Shops at Caesars.

## *Sitting Tall in the Saddle*

# SANDY VALLEY RANCH

**Sandy Valley Rd., Sandy Valley**
**(702) 631-0463 or (877) 726-3998**
**www.sandyvalleyranch.com**

Looking for a real Wild West experience? Take the family trail riding at the Sandy Valley Ranch. The scenery will awe you. The surroundings are not only beautiful, but also a quintessential piece of the Old West. Sitting in the saddle and gazing at the gorgeous mountains on both sides of the valley, you'll swear you hear the theme song from *Bonanza*.

Trail riding's not the only game at the ranch. Sandy Valley also has overnight rides and one- and two-night roundup adventures. Occasionally there's roping, team-penning and just about any other cowboy activity you can think of in the ranch's two arenas.

Families are welcome and parents should be heartened by the fact that ranch managers are particularly education-oriented. They take the time to explain the motivation behind a horse's behavior so novice riders can understand their mounts just a little bit better.

At the end of the trail—or in the middle if you're on a multi-day ride—Big Tony's ready with the grub. Dinner includes everything from country-style ribs and rib-eye steak to catch of the day and vegetarian fajitas. Big Tony's even willing to accommodate dietary needs. If your kids are finicky, let him know in advance.

Then hit the trail!

**SEASONS AND TIMES**

➛ Year-round: Times vary. Call for details.

**COST**

➛ Fees vary. Sunday morning Saddle Club trail rides (2 to 3 hours): $55 per person. Sunset Dinner Trail Rides: $125 per person.

**GETTING THERE**

➛ By car, take I-15 S. to Exit 12 at Jean. Head west on State Rd. 161 to Sandy Valley Rd. Follow this road southwest to the ranch. It's on the south side of the road (the route is well marked). Free parking on site. About 45 minutes from McCarran International Airport.

**NEARBY**

➛ Fashion Outlet at Las Vegas and attractions at Primm.

**COMMENT**

➛ Allow at least 2 to 3 hours for the trail ride and a chance to meet the ranch's other animals.

## *Plane-spotting*
## SUNSET VIEWING AREA

**Near 1200 Sunset Rd. and McCarran International Airport, Las Vegas**
**(702) 261-5211 (General airport information)**
**www.mccarran.com**

Why do residents of Las Vegas watch planes take off and land when they live in the most exciting city in the world? Simple: people find it fascinating. And with one of the busiest international airports in the country, it just adds to the fun.

There's always a lot of excitement in the city when aircraft are on their final approach, lined up in the sky like a new constellation. See if your kids don't share this enthusiasm. During elections and at other times of the year, they might see Air Force One or other VIP aircraft making use of the major east-west runway. Tune your car radio to 88.5 FM and kids can hear radio transmissions between pilots and air-traffic controllers.

Parents should be aware of a somewhat dubious distinction bestowed on the Sunset Viewing Area. It's regularly named as the best make-out spot in town in the *Las Vegas Review-Journal's* Best of Las Vegas contest. You may want to keep the kids' attention diverted from the occupants in the next car.

Families truly dedicated to watching planes can visit the Gus Sabo Memorial Park viewing area at the North Las Vegas Airport. The action's a lot slower, but you can enjoy picnic tables in a park-like setting. It's open only daylight hours.

**SEASONS AND TIMES**

➛ Year-round: Daily, 24 hours.

**COST**

➛ Free.

**GETTING THERE**

➛ By car, take I-215 E. to the Sunset Rd. Exit. Head east on Sunset. The parking area will appear almost immediately on the north side of the road. Located on the edge of McCarran International Airport.

➛ By public transit, take city bus route 212.

**NEARBY**

➛ Sunset Park, All-American Sport Park, Liberace Museum.

**COMMENT**

➛ If you time your visit to the arrival or departure of a VIP, be sure to get there early to beat the crowds—parking is limited.

CHAPTER 11

# FAVORITE FESTIVALS

# *Introduction*

Las Vegas isn't a stronghold for quaint country-style fairs. But the festival hasn't been forgotten in this neon-bedecked city in the desert. Among the most popular are the multi-day craft festivals at Cashman Center. The Great Las Vegas Craft Festival and the Harvest Festival have lots to interest kids, and almost make you forget where you are.

The Pahrump Harvest Festival with its traditional deep-pit barbecue and the classic Clark County Fair are remnants of another era. For a blast from the past, check out the Age of Chivalry Renaissance Festival—the past being around the 15th century. Creativity is celebrated in the Boulder City Art in the Park Festival, and hot air's in the spotlight at the Las Vegas Balloon Festival. Other favorite family festivals include the Greek Food Festival, the Harvest Festival at Red Rock National Conservation Area and last but not least, the Clark County Children's Festival that celebrates our most precious natural resource.

# *Let the Children Play*
# CLARK COUNTY CHILDREN'S FESTIVAL

**Winchester Community Center and Park,**
**3130 S. McLeod Dr., Las Vegas**
**(702) 455-7340**
**www.co.clark.nv.us**

When springtime comes and flowers bloom, parents welcome opportunities to get kids out into the fresh air. A perfect opportunity is the Clark County Children's Festival—an event that lets everyone be a kid.

There's no end to the hands-on and fun-filled offerings at this festival. How do craft workshops, sidewalk chalk drawing or face painting sound to your brood? Wait, there's more. There's also button and musical instrument making, storytelling and historical re-creations for kids to observe. The county Recmobile, with its games and activities, is always a kid favorite. The festival's lineup of cultural activities includes musical performances by young musicians, dancers, steel drum performers and more. For "active" kids there is a bounce house, a swing ride, games and even some kiddie-size carnival rides.

Clark County Children's Festival has won awards for its recreational and cultural offerings. Little wonder: this is a celebration of kids just being kids.

**SEASONS AND TIMES**

➛ Early Mar: Sat. Call the number above or visit the website for exact dates.

**COST**

➛ Free.

**GETTING THERE**

➛ By car, take I-15 N. to the Desert Inn Rd. E. Exit. Head east on Desert Inn to McLeod Dr. and turn north. The park is on the east side of the road. Free parking on site. About 20 minutes from McCarran International Airport.

➛ By public transit, take city bus route 111.

**NEARBY**

➛ Boulevard Mall, the Sahara, Circus Circus.

**COMMENT**

➛ Plan at least a 2-hour visit.

## *Folk Art and More*

# GREAT LAS VEGAS CRAFT FESTIVAL

**Cashman Center, 850 Las Vegas Blvd. N., Las Vegas**
**(702) 386-7184**
**www.vegasfreedom.com/meet-2.asp**

What a way to inspire kids to think creatively. A trip to the semi-annual Great Las Vegas Craft Festival is a chance to see artists and artisans at work.

Event organizers won't allow mass-produced work at this festival. All items on display and offered for sale must be the work of the artisan manning the booth. This festival is large, in recent years featuring 200 booths representing 300 independent artisans from throughout the West. Visitors see pottery, jewelry, fiber arts including weaving, leather, glass, sculpture and woodwork. Of special interest to kids are those artisans who create toys—and there are lots of them producing everything from old-fashioned whirligigs to newfangled gizmos to add color and interest to a kid's room.

But all work and no play would be boring, so event organizers bring in troupes of musicians and magicians to entertain the crowd. It all adds up to a lot of crafty fun—and an inspired (and inspiring) way for families to spend a day.

**SEASONS AND TIMES**

→ Mid-Mar: Fri—Sun. Call the number above or visit the website for exact dates.

**COST**

→ Adults $6, youths (6 to 16) $2, under 6 free.

**GETTING THERE**

→ By car, take I-15 N. to I-515/U.S. 93/U.S. 95 and drive south to the Las Vegas Blvd. Exit. Head north on Las Vegas. The center is on the east side of the street, up a few blocks. On-site pay parking ($3). About 35 minutes from McCarran International Airport.

→ By public transit, take city bus route 401.

**NEARBY**

→ Lied Discovery Children's Museum, Las Vegas Natural History Museum, Old Mormon Fort State Park.

**COMMENT**

→ Plan a 2-hour visit. If the kids are restless, combine this festival with a nearby museum or the Mormon Fort.

# *Giddy Up to* CLARK COUNTY FAIR AND RODEO

**Fairgrounds, State Rd. 169, Logandale**
**(702) 398-3247**
**www.ccfair.com**

A county fair in Las Vegas, neon capital of the world? Well, it's not actually in Las Vegas. The fair's located in Logandale, the part of the county with an agricultural and rural bent.

Looking for county-fair classics? It doesn't get much better than a competition for Rodeo Queen and Princess, children's rodeo (in addition to the adult version) and talent shows for kids and adults. It's got everything any county fair could offer—including racing pigs.

Animals are a big part of every county fair and this one has more than its share. Kids can take in a junior livestock sale, junior market swine show, 4H horse show, sheep fitting contest and junior market lamb show. There are even small animals exhibits where they can get up-close-and-personal with cuddly creatures.

Save some time for the rides at the carnival midway. And be sure to check out the entertainment, including classic country bands. Feeling hungry? Food booths serve all your favorite carnival goodies. It adds up to lots of old-fashioned fun—and a great break from the glitz and glitter.

**SEASONS AND TIMES**

→ Late Mar—early Apr. Call the number above or visit the website for exact dates.

**COST**

→ General admission: Adults $6, seniors $5, children $4. Concert, carnival and rodeo tickets extra.

**GETTING THERE**

→ By car, take I-15 N. to State Rd. 169 (Exit 93). Follow the signs to the fairgrounds in Logandale. Free parking on site. About 45 minutes from McCarran International Airport.

**NEARBY**

→ Lost City Museum, Valley of Fire State Park.

**COMMENT**

→ Plan at least a 3- to 4-hour visit.

*Arts Umbrella*

# HARVEST FESTIVAL

**Cashman Center, 850 Las Vegas Blvd. N., Las Vegas**
**(702) 386-7184**
**www.vegasfreedom.com/meet-2.asp**

The Harvest Festival is first and foremost a craft show. It heralds the coming of autumn with such richness, families look forward to the falling of leaves. It also ensures the kids aren't forgotten. Booths offer temporary tattoos for kids, while others have face painting. A make-it-and-take-it area features finger painting and places where kids can make pins or cards to take home.

In addition to providing diversionary fun for youngsters, these activities give them a feeling for what's going on around them. Mixed in among the fair's 16,000 crafts are all types of goods imaginable—from handmade soap, candles and toys to woodcrafts, gourmet pasta, potpourri, Western art and more. Creative children especially enjoy watching the artists, such as potters and leather workers, demonstrating their skills. Most items are for sale and you can browse all you want.

The festival is designed with active families in mind. There's a parcel check for storing your purchases and changing facilities for those in diapers. A Mexican food booth and deli featuring a baked potato and salsa bar has chairs for dining and resting. Relax a spell and enjoy the continuous musical entertainment. Remember to pick up some fudge for the ride home.

### SEASONS AND TIMES

→ Late Aug: Fri—Sun. Call the number above or visit the website for exact dates.

### COST

→ Adults $6, seniors $5, children (6 to 12) $4, under 6 free. The tickets are good for all three days.

### GETTING THERE

→ By car, take I-15 N. to I-515/U.S. 93/U.S. 95 and drive south to the Las Vegas Blvd. Exit. Head north on Las Vegas. The center is on the east side of the street, up a few blocks. On-site pay parking ($3). About 35 minutes from McCarran International Airport.

→ By public transit, take city bus route 401.

**NEARBY**

➛ Lied Discovery Children's Museum, Las Vegas Natural History Museum, Old Mormon Fort State Park.

**COMMENT**

➛ Plan a 2-hour visit. If the kids are restless, combine this festival with a nearby museum or the Mormon Fort.

## *Going to the Country*
# PAHRUMP HARVEST FESTIVAL AND FAIR

**Petrack Park, Basin Ave. and Hwy. 160, Pahrump**
**(702) 727-5107**
**www.amargosavalley.com/HarvestFest/harvestfestival.html**

Looking for an old-fashioned fall country fair in Southern Nevada? Pahrump may just be the place.

The Pahrump Harvest Festival and Fair, approaching its 40th birthday, has everything a country fair-lovin' family could want. The centerpiece is the annual deep-pit barbecue sponsored by Pahrump Valley Fire and Rescue. If anybody knows how to cook, it's firefighters. These guys start with 5,000 pounds of beef, 160 gallons of barbecue sauce and 15 pounds of garlic. They wrap it in burlap and bury it in the ground with six cords of mesquite wood for just the right sweet tinge. The barbecue is then served up with cowboy beans and the rest of the fixin's, a feast for most of the 10,000 people who drop by each year.

There's more going on than delicious food. The festival has over 200 fair exhibits and old-fashioned pie-eating and greased-pig contests. There's lots of live entertainment and a carnival midway.

Still not impressed? Check out the rodeo sanctioned by the Professional Rodeo Cowboy Association or the races at the Pahrump Valley Speedway. There's also a run and a fun walk everyone can sign up for, and even a church service. The whole package is guaranteed to be good for the soul.

**SEASONS AND TIMES**

➛ Mid-Sept: Fri—Sun. Call the number above or visit the website for exact dates.

**COST**

➛ Free admission. Fees for carnival rides, rodeo and speedway events.

**GETTING THERE**

➛ By car, take I-15 S. to State Rd. 160 (Blue Diamond Rd.) and follow 160 west to Pahrump. The park is on the west side of the street at Basin Ave. Free parking on site. About 1 hour from McCarran International Airport.

**NEARBY**

➛ Pahrump Valley Vineyards, Death Valley National Park.

**COMMENT**

➛ Plan a 3- to 4-hour visit.

# *Tucking In at*
# THE GREEK FOOD FESTIVAL

**St. John the Baptist Church, 5300 El Camino Rd., Las Vegas**
**(702) 221-8245**

"Opa!" That singular Greek exclamation of joy is what the kids will be shouting after a few hours at the Greek Food Festival. Founded in 1972, it is now the city's oldest celebration of food. The festival is held at St. John the Baptist Church and is a love-in of all things Hellenic.

What a way to introduce kids to another cuisine. They can sample dolmathes (stuffed grape leaves), pastitso (layered meat and macaroni) and moussaka (a layered eggplant dish), among other favorites. And don't forget the pastries, including the classic baklava and kourabiedes (butter cookies with powdered sugar).

The weekend-long extravaganza shines the spotlight on other aspects of Greek culture. You can listen to live music by a Greek band, see costumed folk dancers and settle back in a coffee taverna. There's lots to keep the little ones entertained. They can go for pony rides, have their faces painted, attend a bazaar and play organized games.

It's all for a good cause. Proceeds from the festival have helped the parish move to different locations as the congregation has grown. But most of all, it's a lot of fun with tasty food to boot.

### SEASONS AND TIMES
→ Late Sept: Fri—Sun. Call the number above for exact dates.

### COST
→ Admission: Individuals $2, children (12 and younger) free. Extra charge for food and some activities.

### GETTING THERE
→ By car, take I-15 N. to Russell Rd. W. Head west on Russell to Decatur Blvd., then north on Decatur to Hacienda. Turn west onto Hacienda until El Camino. The church is at the intersection of Hacienda and El Camino. Free parking on site. About 20 minutes from McCarran International Airport.
→ By public transit, take city bus route 102.

### NEARBY
→ Chinatown Plaza, The Orleans Hotel-Casino.

### COMMENT
→ Plan at least a 2-hour visit.

# *Art in the Open Air*
# BOULDER CITY ART IN THE PARK FESTIVAL

**Bicentennial Park, Utah and Colorado streets, Boulder City**
**(702) 294-1611 (Boulder City Hospital Auxiliary)**
**www.riverlakes.com/BCevents.htm**

Boulder City is devoted to history and the arts. And the arts are in the spotlight during the city's Art in the Park Festival held each October.

A local schoolteacher started the festival in 1962 as a benefit for the Boulder City Hospital Auxiliary. It was first held in the tiny backyard of one of its members. Now approaching its 40th year, this much-anticipated event has grown to encompass more than 300 booths.

Featured are fine arts and crafts including clothing, ceramics, wood, jewelry, pottery and sculpture. It's a juried show, so you aren't likely to find things made out of old soft-drink bottles. The festival's still a fund-raiser for the hospital auxiliary and annually raises more than $100,000.

Food booths are part of the picture, offering such kid-pleasing treats as pizza and ice cream. While youngsters may get bored walking up and down the aisles of booths, they'll be fascinated seeing the occasional artist at work and sharing the secrets of their creative endeavors. If all else fails,

Bicentennial Park offers playground equipment where kids can let off some steam.

**SEASONS AND TIMES**

➛ Early Oct: Sat—Sun. Call the number above or visit the website for exact dates.

**COST**

➛ Admission is free. Charge for the food.

**GETTING THERE**

➛ By car, take I-215 E. to its end. Proceed east on Lake Mead Dr. to I-515/U.S. 93/U.S. 95 and go south to Boulder City. At the U.S. 93 fork, follow Nevada Hwy. to Bicentennial Park. It is on the south side of the road, up several blocks. Parking at Boulder City Airport (shuttle provided), $2 per car. To reach the airport, turn south at the U.S. 93 fork onto Buchanan; the airport will be on the west side, about 1 1/2 miles down the road. About 50 minutes from McCarran International Airport.

➛ By public transit, take city bus route 116.

**NEARBY**

➛ Hoover Dam, Lake Mead National Recreation Area.

**COMMENT**

➛ Plan at least a 2-hour visit. Consider combining this with Hoover Dam, Boulder City-Hoover Dam Museum, or Boulder City Historic District.

# *Milords and Ladies*
# AGE OF CHIVALRY RENAISSANCE FESTIVAL

**Sunset Park, 2601 E. Sunset Rd., Las Vegas**
**(702) 455-8200**

Chivalry is dead? Tell that to the mobs who attend this annual festival. More than 4,000 participants and 50,000 festival-go'ers gather each year at Sunset Park to celebrate the bright spots of the Dark Ages. The festival is an eye-opener for youngsters whose passion is knights and fairy tale castles. It's two full days of jousting tournaments, performances of Shakespeare's works, riding demonstrations, royal parades, musical performances and even a "fight" between British and Scottish troops in the Battle of Sunset Park. Bands of wandering minstrels, story-tellers, magicians and dancers delight and amuse. Tell your kids to keep their eyes open for the fire-eater.

And while the festival-go'ers are milling around in shorts and T-shirts, participants and avid fans wear Renaissance garb, some of it amazingly ornate. The local chapter of the Society for Creative Anachronism takes part and adds much color to the festivities.

Don't forget the food. While wandering around the site looking at the medieval toys and clothing articles for sale, kids can munch on a smoked turkey leg à la King Henry VIII. Foods that were everyday fare during the period from the 12th through the 15th centuries are on the menu.

**SEASONS AND TIMES**

→ Mid-Oct: Sat—Sun (schools-only day on Friday). Call the number above for exact dates.

**COST**

→ Adults $7, seniors, members of the military and children (5 to 12) $5, under 5 free.

**GETTING THERE**

→ By car, take I-215 E. to the Sunset Rd. Exit and head east on Sunset. The park will be on the south side of the road at the next major intersection. Free parking on site. About 10 minutes from McCarran International Airport.

→ By public transit, take city bus route 212.

**NEARBY**

→ All-American SportPark, Liberace Museum.

**COMMENT**

→ Plan at least a 3- to 4-hour visit. Sunset Park (page 155) offers visitors an array of other entertaining options.

# *Celebrating Nature*
# HARVEST FESTIVAL

**Red Rock Canyon, State Rd. 159, Las Vegas**
**(702) 363-1921**
**www.redrockcanyon.blm.gov/default.htm**

Red Rock Canyon National Conservation Area is a common secret for residents and frequent visitors to Las Vegas. Casual observers have no idea that a place with this much natural beauty exists close to the city.

And to celebrate the natural beauty of the region, Red Rock has been throwing a Harvest Festival for several years. It's a true family affair with crafts for kids and a chance to meet Smokey the Bear™ and Woodsey Owl™. The cultures of the area's Native peoples are also celebrated with demonstrations of such arts as pine-needle basketry and gourd decorating.

Organizers never forget the animals. Local wildlife is included by way of presentations of wild-horse and burro adoptions by the Bureau of Land Management, plus displays of venomous and non-venomous snakes that inhabit the area. The Las Vegas Metropolitan Police Department is on hand with demonstrations by its search-and-rescue team—both career inspiration for the kids and a living admonition to keep away from the canyon's more hazardous areas.

Like Red Rock itself, word is spreading about the festival. While only a few hundred people attended in the festival's first year, recent years' attendance has been up in the thousands.

**SEASONS AND TIMES**

→ Mid-Oct: Sat. Call the number above or visit the website for exact dates.

**COST**

→ Regular $5 per car park entry fee.

**GETTING THERE**

→ By car, take I-15 S. to the State Rd. 160 (Blue Diamond Rd.) Exit. Follow 160 west to its intersection with State Rd. 159. Head north on 159; Red Rock will be about 7 miles down the road on the west side. Free parking on site. About 35 minutes from McCarran International Airport.

**NEARBY**

→ Spring Mountain Ranch State Park, Bonnie Springs.

**COMMENT**

→ Plan a 2-hour visit. Consider combining this with a picnic at Spring Mountain Ranch or dinner at Bonnie Springs.

# *Up, Up and Away at* LAS VEGAS BALLOON CLASSIC

**Silver Bowl Park (adjacent to Sam Boyd Stadium), 6800 E. Russell Rd., Las Vegas**
**(702) 895-3900**

Like the Energizer Bunny™, the Las Vegas Balloon Classic just keeps going and going. The bunny has a stake in the three-day festival, now in its third decade.

It's one of the corporate icons whose form has inspired the shapes of the balloons on display. Between the inflated bunny and a 55-foot-wide Burger King Whopper™, what kid could resist? This classic features nearly 65 hot-air craft and routinely attracts balloon enthusiasts from all over the world, including New Zealand and Great Britain.

Get to the park early in the morning if you want to see the balloons lift off and fill the sky with their gentle dabs of color. Other balloon-related events are featured too, including the Hare and Hound. One balloon—representing the hare—lifts off before the others and drops a target for them to aim for. The Saturday evening Balloon Glow features illuminated balloons in the night sky. It's a spectacle everyone should see.

Rounding out the event are hot-air balloon rides (regular and tethered, both for an extra fee); horse, pony and horse-drawn wagon rides; panning for gold; a petting zoo; a chili cook-off; arts and crafts booths; car displays; food and more. But for most kids, it's enough to gaze upon those smudges of color hanging lazily in the sky and dream about the day when they can ride in a beautiful balloon.

**SEASONS AND TIMES**

➛ Late Oct: Fri–Sun. Call the number above for exact dates.

**COST**

➛ Admission free. Charges for certain activities and food.

**GETTING THERE**

➛ By car, take I-215 E. to its end. Then follow Lake Mead Dr. to Boulder Hwy. and turn north. The park and stadium are on the east side of the road at the Russell Rd. intersection. Free parking on site. About 40 minutes from McCarran International Airport.
By public transit, take city bus route 107.

**COMMENT**

➛ Plan at least a 2- to 3-hour visit.

# KID-FRIENDLY RESTAURANTS

Eating out with the family offers numerous rewards, chief among them that someone else does the cooking and dishes. Luckily, there is no shortage of restaurants in the Las Vegas area that welcome families. Each offers a fun atmosphere, good food that's reasonably priced and the staff is friendly. Buffets are a particularly popular Las Vegas family option because they offer varied selections, quick service, budget prices and kids get to choose their own food.

Most of the restaurants listed below offer kids' menus or kid-sized portions upon request, booster and high chairs, crayons and paper to keep little hands occupied. Many accommodate nursing moms, too, and provide baby changing stations.

## Buca di Beppo

**(Family-style Italian; raucous atmosphere; crayons and coloring books)**

**7690 W. Lake Mead Blvd., Las Vegas (702) 363-6524**

**412 E. Flamingo Rd., Las Vegas (702) 866-2867**

## Carrabba's Italian Grill

(Kids' menu; crayons; bead toys; dough for sculpting)
10160 S. Eastern Ave., Henderson (702) 990-0650

## Chili's Grill & Bar

(Kids' menu; coloring books)
2520 S. Decatur Blvd., Las Vegas (702) 871-0500
2011 N. Rainbow Blvd., Las Vegas (702) 638-1482
2751 N. Green Valley Pkwy., Henderson (702) 433-3333

## Chuck E. Cheese's

(Birthday parties; games and rides; animated show; cheesy pizza)
7381 W. Lake Mead Blvd., Las Vegas (702) 243-9944
1521 Sunset Rd., Henderson (702) 547-0059

## Di Martino's Your Neighborhood Italian Eatery

(Kids' menu; Etch-a-Sketches™)
1000 N. Green Valley Pkwy., Henderson (702) 269-7144

## 5 & Diner

(Kids' menu; coloring and crayons; great shakes; 1950s decor)
375 N. Stephanie St., Henderson (702) 940-2050
1900 N. Buffalo Dr., Las Vegas (702) 233-5083
6840 W. Sahara Ave., Las Vegas (702) 368-7903
8820 S. Eastern Ave., Las Vegas (702) 966-2650

## Joe's Crab Shack

(Nightly visits from a balloon lady; kids' menu; crayons)
4250 E. Sunset Rd., Henderson (702) 990-2001
1991 N. Rainbow Blvd., Las Vegas (702) 646-3996
9440 W. Sahara Ave., Las Vegas (702) 240-6055

## Landry's Seafood House

(Kids' menu; coloring book)
2610 W. Sahara Ave., Las Vegas (702) 251-0101

## Macayo Vegas
(Mexican food; casual setting; kids' menu; coloring and crayons)
1741 E. Charleston Blvd., Las Vegas (702) 382-5605
4457 W. Charleston Blvd., Las Vegas (702) 878-7347
1375 E. Tropicana Blvd., Las Vegas (702) 736-1898

## Memphis Championship Barbecue
(Kids' menu; ice-cream drinks; crayons)
2130 E. Warm Springs Rd., Las Vegas (702) 260-6909
4379 Las Vegas Blvd. N., Las Vegas (702) 644-0000

## NASCAR Cafe
(Kids' menu; cars and racing memorabilia)
Sahara Hotel and Casino, 2535 Las Vegas Blvd. S., Las Vegas (702) 734-7223

## Old Spaghetti Factory
(Kids' menu; crayons)
721 Mall Ring Circle, Henderson (702) 458-0845

## Peppermill Inn Restaurant
(Kids' menu; activity book; dining under big flowering trees)
2985 Las Vegas Blvd. S., Las Vegas (702) 735-4177

## Race Rock
(Kids' menu; monster trucks, race cars, race boats and race memorabilia on display; racing videos)
425 Fremont St., Las Vegas (702) 382-7223

## Rainforest Café
(Kids' menu; birthday parties; coloring books; jungle atmosphere)
MGM Grand Hotel/Casino, 3799 Las Vegas Blvd. S., Las Vegas (702) 891-8580

## Red Robin
(Visits from the Red Robin; kids' menu; coloring and crayons; balloons; games)
1300 W. Sunset Road, Henderson (702) 547-1777

**2575 S. Decatur Blvd., Las Vegas (702) 364-1858**
**151 N. Nellis Blvd., Las Vegas (702) 453-8611**

## Roadhouse Grill

(Kids' menu; balloons; Etch-a-Sketches™; kids can throw the peanut shells on the floor)
**521 Stephanie St., Henderson (702) 456-7405**
**4945 W. Tropicana Ave., Las Vegas (702) 222-0846**
**7341 W. Lake Mead Blvd., Las Vegas (702) 256-2755**

## Romano's Macaroni Grill

(Kids' menu; coloring and crayons; games)
**2400 W. Sahara Ave., Las Vegas (702) 248-9500**
**2001 N. Rainbow Blvd., Las Vegas (702) 648-6688**
**573 Stephanie St., Henderson (702) 433-2788**

## Star Trek: The Experience, Quark's Bar & Restaurant

(Kids' menu; space-age atmosphere; costumed Trekkies strolling around)
**Las Vegas Hilton, 3000 Paradise Rd., Las Vegas (702) 697-8700**

## Tony Roma's

(Coloring book; kids' menu; crayons)
**555 Stephanie St., Henderson (702) 436-2227**
**620 E. Sahara Ave., Las Vegas (702) 733-9914**
**2040 N. Rainbow Blvd., Las Vegas (702) 638-2100**
**200 Fremont St., Las Vegas (702) 385-6257**

# FAMILY-FRIENDLY HOTELS

Looking for home-away-from-home comfort when you are on vacation? Face it, staying at a hotel can be hectic when you're traveling as a family. New surroundings, an unfamiliar bed—it can unsettle even the most adventurous child. Whether your stay in Las Vegas is a few days or a couple of weeks, the family-friendly establishments below will make sure your brood wakes up refreshed and ready to take on a new day.

In addition to providing a relaxed atmosphere, most have services for families, from babysitting and kids' clubs to games rooms and more. Some of these hotels offer family discounts, too.

## *Value*

### Circus Circus Hotel, Casino & Theme Park

**(Under 18 stay free; free circus acts; pay theme park; arcade games; pool; food court)**
**2880 Las Vegas Blvd., Las Vegas (702) 734-0410**

### Fitzgeralds Casino & Holiday Inn

**(Under 19 stay free; free nightly light-and-sound shows; under 13 eat free from room-service menu when an adult orders)**
**301 Fremont St., Las Vegas (702) 388-2400**

## *Moderate*

### Boulder Station Hotel-Casino

**(Under 14 stay free; child-care center; movie theater; arcade games; pool; food court)**
**4111 Boulder Hwy., Las Vegas (702) 432-7777**

### Excalibur Hotel & Casino

(Under 14 stay free; dinner show; arcade games; pool; food court)
3850 Las Vegas Blvd. S., Las Vegas (702) 597-7777

### Luxor Las Vegas

(Under 12 stay free; 3-D Imax™ theater; motion-simulator rides; King Tut museum; arcade games; pool; food court)
3900 Las Vegas Blvd. S., Las Vegas (702) 262-4444

### Sam's Town Hotel & Gambling Hall

(Under 13 stay free; free laser light and fountain show; supervised child-care center; movie theater; arcade games; bowling alley; pool; food court; RV park)
5111 Boulder Hwy., Las Vegas (702) 456-7777

### Sunset Station Hotel & Casino

(Under 14 stay free; supervised child-care center; movie theater; arcade games; pool; food court)
1301 W. Sunset Rd., Henderson (702) 547-7777

### Texas Station Gambling Hall & Hotel

(Under 14 stay free; supervised child-care center; movie theater; arcade games; bowling alley; pool; food court)
2101 Texas Star Lane, North Las Vegas (702) 631-1000

## *Expensive*

### MGM Grand Hotel, Casino & Theme Park

(Under 13 stay free; pay seasonal theme park; supervised child-care center; free lion-habitat exhibit; arcade games; pool; food court; Rainforest Café)
3799 Las Vegas Blvd. S., Las Vegas (702) 891-1111

### The Mirage

(Under 3 stay free; free white tiger exhibit; dolphin habitat; Secret Garden of Siegfried & Roy; arcade games; pool; food court)
3400 Las Vegas Blvd. S., Las Vegas (702) 791-7111

# 12 *Months of Fun*
# DIRECTORY OF EVENTS

**JANUARY**

**Mid-January**
Martin Luther King Jr. Parade
Downtown Las Vegas
(702) 629-6011

**Late January to early February**
Chinese New Year
China Town Plaza
(702) 248-9705

**FEBRUARY**

**Early February to early April**
Las Vegas Outlaws XFL team
Sam Boyd Stadium
(702) 24BLITZ (242-5489)

**MARCH**

**Early March**
Clark County Children's Festival
Winchester Community Center
and Park
(702) 455-7340

**Early March**
Komen Las Vegas Race for the
Cure
Galleria at Sunset, Henderson
(702) 252-RACE (7223)

**Early March**
NASCAR Winston Cup Stock Car
Races
Las Vegas Motor Speedway
(702) 644-4444

**Mid-March**
Great Las Vegas Craft Festival
Cashman Center
(702) 386-7184

**Mid-March**
St. Patrick's Day Parade
Downtown Las Vegas
(702) 629-6011

**Late March to early April**
Clark County Fair and Rodeo
Fairgrounds, Logandale
(702) 398-3247

**APRIL**

**Early April**
Winston NHRA Drag Racing
Series
Las Vegas Motor Speedway
(702) 644-4444

**Early April**
Foreign Language Fair
Las Vegas Academy
(702) 799-7800

**Early April**
Laughlin River Stampede
Laughlin
(800) 4LAUGHLIN (452-8445)

**Mid-April to late September**
Las Vegas 51s baseball
Cashman Field
(702) 386-7200

**Late April**
Indy Racing League/NASCAR
Winston West
Las Vegas Motor Speedway
(702) 644-4444

**Late April**
BET on Jazz, Las Vegas City of
Lights Jazz Festival
Hills Park
(702) 228-3780

**MAY**

**Early May**
Cinco de Mayo Festival
Lorenzi Park
(702) 229-6729

**Early May**
Craft Fair, Rib Burn-Off and Car Show
Sunset Park
(702) 455-8200

**Early May**
Make Strides Against Breast Cancer Walk
Paseo Verde Park, Henderson
(702) 798-6877

**Mid-May**
Race and Fun Run
Cashman Center
(702) 737-1919

**Late May**
Israel Independence Festival
University of Nevada
(702) 732-0556

**Late May**
Jaycees Blues Festival
Lorenzi Park
(702) 229-6729

**Late May to late June**
Jazz in the Park Concert Series
Clark County Government Center amphitheatre
(702) 455-8200

**JUNE**

**Early June**
Las Vegas Jazz Festival at the Fremont Street Experience
Fremont Street Experience
(702) 678-5600

**Early June**
Laughlin River Days Formula One Racing
Colorado River, Laughlin
(800) 4LAUGHLIN (452-8445)

**June to late August**
Super Summer Theater
Spring Mountain Ranch State Park
(702) 875-4141

**JULY**

**Thursdays in July**
Family Film Festival
Jaycee Park
(702) 229-6211

**July 4**
Independence Day Fireworks
Various locations around Las Vegas
(702) 892-0711

**July 4**
Summerlin 4th of July Fest
Summerlin
(702) 341-5500

**Early July**
Ringling Bros. and Barnum & Bailey Circus
Thomas & Mack Center
(702) 895-UNLV (8658)

**AUGUST**

**Early August**
Las Vegas Music Festival
University of Nevada
(702) 895-2787

**Late August**
Harvest Festival
Cashman Center
(702) 386-7184

**Late August**
Liberace Scholars Festival of the Arts
Clark County Library Theater
(702) 798-5595

**SEPTEMBER**

**Tuesdays in September**
Latin Film Festival
Charleston Heights Arts Center
(702) 229-6383

**Early September to late December**
UNLV football
Sam Boyd Stadium
(702) 895-UNLV (8658)

**Mid-September**
Pahrump Harvest Festival and Fair
Petrack Park
(702) 727-5107

**Mid-September to mid-May**
Las Vegas Philharmonic
University of Nevada
(702) 895-ARTS (2787)

**Late September**
Greek Food Festival
St. John the Baptist Greek Orthodox Church
(702) 221-8245

**Late September**
All-You-Can-Eat Ice Cream Festival
Willows Park
(702) 791-4500

**Late September**
Blue Sky International Film Festival
Sunset Station
(702) 737-3313

**OCTOBER**

**Early October**
Boulder City Art in the Park Festival
Bicentennial Park, Boulder City
(702) 294-1611

**Early October**
Nevada Shakespeare in the Park
Foxridge Park, Henderson
(702) 566-2681

**Early October**
Pahrump Fat Tire Festival
Pahrump
(775) 727-5800

**Mid-October**
Age of Chivalry Renaissance Festival
Sunset Park
(702) 455-8200

**Mid-October**
Harvest Festival
Red Rock Canyon National Conservation Area
(702) 363-1921

**Mid-October**
Zelzah Shrine Circus
Sunset Station
(702) 382-5554

**Mid-October to mid-May**
Rainbow Company Children's Theatre
Charleston Heights Arts Center
(702) 229-6553

**Late October**
Las Vegas Hot-Air Balloon & Kite Festival
Desert Breeze Park
(702) 455-8334

**Late October**
Las Vegas Balloon Classic
Silver Bowl Park
(702) 895-3900

**Late October**
Winston NHRA Drag Racing Series
Las Vegas Motor Speedway
(702) 644-4444

## NOVEMBER

**Early November to early March**
UNLV men's and women's basketball
Thomas & Mack Center
(702) 895-UNLV (8658)

**Nov. 11**
Veterans Day Parade
Downtown Las Vegas
(702) 629-6011

**Mid-November**
Great Craft Festival
Cashman Center
(702) 386-7184

**Late November**
Festival of Trees and Light
Paris, Las Vegas
(702) 946-7000

**Late November to late December**
Magical Forest
Opportunity Village
(702) 259-3700

## DECEMBER

**Early December**
CineVegas International Film Festival
Paris, Las Vegas
(877) 374-7469

**Early December**
Las Vegas Tree-lighting Ceremony
Fremont Street Experience
(702) 678-5600

**Early December**
National Finals Rodeo
Thomas & Mack Center
(702) 895-3500

**Early December**
Parade of Lights
Lake Mead
(702) 293-8907

**Mid-December**
Henderson Tree-lighting Ceremony
Henderson Convention Center, Henderson
(702) 566-2289

**Mid-December**
Menorah-lighting ceremony
Fremont Street Experience
(702) 678-5600

**Mid-December**
Hanukkah Celebration
Galleria at Sunset
(702) 434-0202

# INDEX

# THE LOBSTER KIDS' CITY EXPLORERS SERIES

**$12.95 US • $17.95 CDN**

*The Lobster Kids' Guide to Exploring*

**CALGARY**

By Kate Zimmerman with Diane Thuna

ISBN 1-894222-08-3

*The Lobster Kids' Guide to Exploring*

**MONTRÉAL**

By John Symon

Revised Edition

ISBN 1-894222-09-1

*The Lobster Kids' Guide to Exploring*

**TORONTO**

By Nathalie Ann Comeau

ISBN 1-894222-07-5

*The Lobster Kids' Guide to Exploring*

**VANCOUVER**

By Jeni Wright

ISBN 1-894222-05-9

*The Lobster Kids' Guide to Exploring*

**OTTAWA-HULL**

By John Symon

ISBN 1-894222-01-6

$12.95 US • $16.95 CDN

**Available in all bookstores or order from www.lobsterpress.com**